CXC

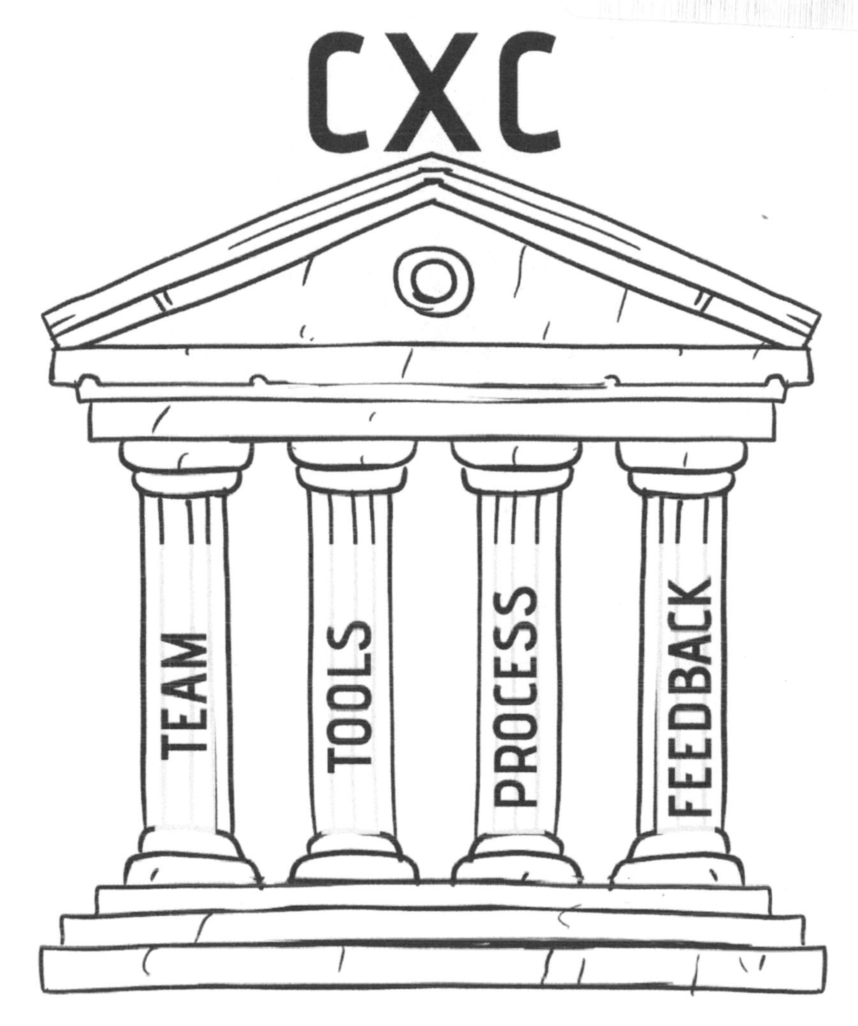

The 4 CX Pillars To Grow Your Business

By ADRIAN BRADY-CESANA

The Four CX Pillars™

The Customer Experience Manager Playbook

By Adrian Brady-Cesana

Founder & Chief Experience Officer @ CXChronicles

Table of Contents

Acknowledgements

With the intent of starting things off with positive juju, I'd like to thank everyone who supported me throughout this book-writing journey over the course of an entire year.

To my family: The love of my life, Ashlee, who has been one of my biggest champions in life and building CXC; My parents, Tish & Paul, who encouraged me to write; My older and *cough, cough* wiser brother, Dax, sister-in-law and side-hustle expert, Elissa, my future boss lady niece, Elle, and the late wolves, Halley and Brody.

To my best friends: Ry & Charlie Sunday from Lotus Bay, USA and Cousin Jeffrey for always helping me keep things in perspective and calling out my pure love for black polos and ninja socks - everyday, every season, always and forever.

To the rest of the Lakeshore & PSU crew: Keep on shakin' 'em! Special thanks to Kurt Wojda, who helped me with the book cover and graphic design to get this book up on the shelves for all of you to notice and actually pick up and read. And to my PSU gang of north country buds - here's to always taking the three, regardless of the down at hand!

To the CXNation: Thanks for listening to our podcast and following other CXC content that we've put out over the past two years. We've seen thousands of podcast downloads, a growing listenership and we've connected with hundreds of global industry leading CX experts who are all looking forward to adding this book to their CX library.

I hope that this book makes all of you proud, adds tons of value to your business and guides you to make happiness a habit!

About Me

The last thing I ever thought I would do is write a book before the age of 30. Well, that in fact never happened because, as I crossed the final t's and dotted the final lowercase j's for this book, I was a nice, ripe age of 34-years-old.

To be perfectly honest, when I was younger I hated the idea of writing books for one simple reason: my parents always told me. "You should write books and travel the world giving speeches," they would say.

"Fuck that noise!" adolescent Adrian thought. Who wants to listen to their parents when they're that age anyways? Like any average suburban teenager, I dreamed of becoming a rockstar, playing the drums in an internationally known rock 'n' roll band touring the world, getting banged up (definitely a little weird), and making millions selling albums.

Then this thing we call 'life' rolled red-hot with brakes screeching into the stationand made its own plans for me. Needless to say, what I had mapped out at age 16 was certainly not played out. In fact, 16-year-old me would actually be pissed and kick my adult-ass if he knew I grew "soft" and enjoyed helping businesses grow through the power of incredible customer experiences. Teenage Adrian would've definitely labeled that as "lame."

Before my life in customer experience began, I spent my college years in the Adirondack Mountains of New York in a beautiful, north country town called Plattsburgh. I spent most of our "North Country" college years listening to live music at the Monopole, eating Zuke's for lunch, heading out to breakfast at Guma's on the weekends and riding most of the winter at Jay Peak resort in Vermont. After graduation, I jumped into a variety of small family-owned businesses back in my hometown of Buffalo, New York. I immediately took to the task that most fellow employees dreaded: managing client relationships.

Most of my early teammates and colleagues hated dealing with customer issues. I actually liked it and honestly, was really good at it. To me, it was simple:make them think you care - even better, actually care, figure out what is bothering them and do it with a smile.Now that I write that, it's probably where my mantra of "Make Happiness a Habit" comes from.

Quick Exercise: Take a moment and think about what truly makes you happy, what brings you joy. Something that no matter what else is going on in your life, puts you at peace. Now, take it a step further and gradulately spend time each day doing that or those things - even starting out with five minutes can make a difference! Before you know it, you've made happiness a habit!

After spending my first few years out of college in the Buffalo real estate industry, I was quite versed in my customer service and customer interaction skills. This led me to my first big break and figurative knock at the door!

The company that I was working for at the time had an opportunity to expand their services to the Central Florida area for one of our existing national clients. I jumped at the chance: took the $10,000.00 I had saved living with my folks, bought a silver 2004 Ford 150 FX4, loaded up my two labradors (Halley and Brody) and started cruising down south to Florida.

This was it! The beginning of my 15-year (and going) entrepreneurial journey: my very own company.

Introduction

In grade school, I remember a textbook rule to always address "The 5 Ws & H." I figured we'd check those boxes right off the bat to help set the stage.

Who is this book for?

I could go the easy route and say this book was written for customer-facing professionals, but honestly, it's for anyone who has an impact on a business. Whether you're the administrative assistant who directs calls, the engineer who builds new features, the chef who prepares dinner, the executive who manages teams, you all have an effect on the customer journey.

This book is for those who hope to learn more about customer experience, customer service and modern selling in today's world. More importantly, how to make them *dolla dolla bills y'all* - but in all seriousness having thoughtful customer experience (CX) & customer service will only help your business separate itself from the rest of the pack!

CX has become a hot topic over the past ten years as more C-suites tout that they are "customer-centric," "customer focused," "customer-geared," "customer-minded," or whatever other flowery term some good-looking, talking head says on Bloomberg or Squawk Box. Some mean it and walk the walk, and some are blowing smoke up your ass as they lead companies with notoriously poor customer service - *cough cough* airline and cable leaders.

This book is for anyone interested in business and entrepreneurism. Ideal readers include:

- Startup Founders
- Business Owners
- Executives
- Team and Department Heads and Managers
- Investors
- Future Business Leaders (i.e. business students)
- Customer Experience Associates
- Individuals interested in modern business practices, technology and startups
- 10M+ Americans currently working in sales, customer experience and service
- And Customers, who are curious about customer service and design -- remember without customers you have nothing, but a hobby!

My hope is the information and context in this book will provide the "CX Nation" (for The CXChronicles Podcast audience, you know I am talking to you) with a new medium to learn and improve their personal toolkits, increase their chances of making more money, get that bigger, better role and, most importantly, help grow their business through the power of customer experience.

What is CXChronicles?

For those of you who don't know about CXChronicles or The CXChronicles Podcast - they are the companies that I founded in 2018. CXChronicles works with startup and growth focused companies and leadership teams on optimizing The Four CX Pillars™:
Team, Tools, Process and Feedback.

These companies of mine work with clients who see the immediate need to double down their investments in their customer experience design space. CXChronicles provides customer experience training and design, customer journey maps, customized customer feedback strategies or even continuous improvement around the customer operations and inside sales arenas when scaling your startup or growth focused business.

The CXChronicles Podcast is a weekly show (www.CXChronicles.com) that speaks with customer minded business leaders from all over the world, running point as chief customer advocates for their given company or leadership team.

In 2019, Feedspot named our podcast one of the 'Top 15 Customer Service Podcast & Radio Shows to Subscribe and Listen To.' Our guests continue to line up for awesome episodes and we continue to see The CX Nation grow every week. If you haven't had a chance to listen, please sign up and subscribe today on Itune, Spotify, Stitcher or our website.

It's pretty simple. Business leaders who have a firm grasp and understanding of The Four CX Pillars™ are going to make more money, keep their clients longer, develop happier customer experience and service teams, and create more value and ultimately more profits!

When am I writing this book?

As you could imagine, it takes time to write your first book and as they say, timing is everything. The perfect time for me started in the fall of 2017, when my mind was clear and stress levels were low (thanks to a recent sabbatical in Southeast Asia and Europe with my future wife)!

I was launching CXChronicles and I knew that writing a book on all of the subject matter points that I had been intimately related to throughout my career would do nothing but help me cement my own CX school of thought. And on top of continuing to develop my own personal CX playbook for success, I could help others as they go through their own personal CX journeys!

Buffalo, NY

Where I wrote this book?

After nearly ten years in New York City, I decided to move away from the hustle and bustle of the concrete jungle to a much quieter, calmer downtown Buffalo, New York with my partner-in-crime, Ashlee.

Moving back to my hometown has served as an incredible motivator in finishing this book. It's allowed me to re-establish connections with my family, friends and other folks from my youth whom I have not seen in a very long time. In a beautiful way, it has helped reset my priorities and expectations in life.. There's simply more to life than getting up each and every day and entering the rat-race, especially if you dislike what you do. It's ok to go outside the box and get creative folks -there are endless ways to make your dolla dolla bills, it's part of the beauty in the modern world!

Buffalo has an incredibly rich history with ties to hundreds of notable creators as:

- Mark Twain: "The father of American literature"
- F. Scott Fitzgerald: The American fiction writer known best for *The Great Gatsby*
- Wolf Blitzer: German-American journalist for CNN
- Frederick Law Olmsted: American landscape architect, who co-designed Central Park and Delaware Park
- Rick James: "I'm Rick James B*TCH!"
- Tim Russert: American television journalist and Buffalo-native
- Millard Fillmore: 13th president of the United States
- Grover Cleveland: 22nd and 24th president of the United States

- The Goo Goo Dolls: American rock band formed in 1986 in Buffalo
- Ani DiFranco: American singer/songwriter and Buffalo-native
- Wiliam Finchter: American actor
- William G. Fargo: Pioneer American expressman who co-founded American Express Company and Wells Fargo
- Rob Gronkowski: former American football tight end, who (unfortunately) played for the New England Patriots

With all this creative and entrepreneurial mojo floating in the air (or maybe it's the smell of Cheerios from the General Mills plant in the morning), I was rejuvenated and able to focus on the foundation and growth of CXChronicles.

Why am I writing this book?

This book was written for a few primary reasons:

- To share the valuable lessons that I've learned while building, managing and scaling several customer experience, customer service, sales and operation teams at high-growth startups.
- To teach and train how to offer the best customer experience.
- To shine a light on the world of customer experience and service optimization through The Four CX Pillars™. I will dive more into this in Chapter Two, but in short, it is a way to focus your lenses on CX through every aspect of your business.

This book will share my findings from 15 plus years in customer-facing roles, as well as my experience at several VC-backed, NYC startups. My roles ranged from:

- General Manager of H. Bloom: One of the world's fastest growing floral subscription companies. I was running one NYC's leading floral design & delivery operations for global accounts.
- Head of Customer Experience for NYC at London-based Onefinestay: A white-glove Airbnb platform that served the rich and famous during their extended vacations before its acquisition for $170M by Accor Hotel Group
- General Manager and Head of Customer Operations at Hometeam: One of the world's hottest home healthcare technology companies, creating beautiful day's for older adults and empowering caregivers while giving them a strong voice through technology.
- Head of Customer Experience at ACV Auctions: An explosive automotive auction that tipped the automotive world on its head by running live auctions every minute of everyday connecting buyers and sellers across the world. Not to mention becoming Buffalo, NY's first crowned "unicorn" being valued at nearly $1.5 billion in 2020.

Surrounding and in between those bullets, I launched a number of my own companies across a variety of industries including: marketing, real estate, food & beverage, house cleaning services, home sharing, podcasts and international clothing companies. Specifically (in order from first to most recent):

- RPM (Rapid Performance Marketing)
- Property Armor LLC
- Evergreen Field Services
- Maids of Manhattan
- NJ Real Estate Specialists
- American Buddha Co. (my ongoing side hustle and future non-profit)
- WNYCatering
- WNYBnB (my real estate holdings)
- Lotus Bay Ventures (my business holdings)
- Most recently, CXChronicles and The CXChronicles Podcast - a customer experience and service consulting agency and network focused on helping business owners and executives improve their overall customer experience.

Each one of these companies and business models were very different and uniquely built for their specific industry types. The one thing that they all had in common was their focus and prioritization of delivering an impeccable customer experience. Working with this variety of teams and industries has provided me with a wide range of perspectives and practices in the customer service space. Through this book, I hope to bring the core values that have helped me grow in the customer service arena as a leader, manager, and team member.

Within each of these organizations, I worked hand-in-hand with the customer experience, customer service, inside & outside sales, and account management teams composed of remarkable teammates who put the customer first each and every day, no matter the severity and complexity of the challenges presented!

(With my teammate, Evan Frankel, in the NYC floral studio @ H.Bloom 2012)

(With my teammate, Jordan Quitko, in the Hometeam HQ in NYC 2016 - as seen in The Muse)

How This Book Will Help You Grow Your Business?

Being customer experience focused is on the rise and The Four CX Pillars™ provide a strong foundation for business leaders, executives, and entrepreneurs to plan ahead and strategize for the future.

Customer experience is modern selling, don't ever forget that! Ensuring that customer churn is limited to null, and focusing on building a stable of repeat customers adds tons of current and future value and longevity of any business large or small. Focusing on strengthening The Four CX Pillars™ for your company is a sure way to bring lasting success and increase your profits into the future!

As we proceed through each chapter, I will share how to hone your customer-focused craft and refining your individual style through these avenues:

- CXChronicle's The Four CX Pillars™ Methodology (Team, Tools, Process and Feedback) to grow your business, regardless of size or industry
- CXChronicles primary products to help grow your business include the following:
    - CX Scorecards: Evaluate and assess The Four CX Pillars™
    - CX Roadmaps: Build your CX strategy
    - CX Implementation Plans: Optimize The Four CX Pillars™
    - Customer Experience Manager Training: Develop your management and leadership teams to increase your organizational awareness around CX
    - Customer Experience Manager-In-a-Box: Design and build playbooks, process maps, tool roll-outs, etc.
    - CXC Training Videos: Learn The Four CX Pillars™ via virtual lessons
- Customer Experience Optimization: How historical data correlates to previous focus areas, such as Search Engine Optimization (SEO) or User Experience (UX)
- Team Building: Advance your company's sales, customer experience and customer service teams
- Churn Mitigation: Learn from your former customers and become proactive
- Voice of the Customer (VOC): Conduct customer voice exercises for your business and manage customer feedback constantly

CHAPTER ONE

Customer Experience and Service in Today´s World

1

Customer Experience and Service in Today´s World

When thinking about "classic customer service" the majority of us have relied on the telephone or in-person communication to connect with companies when there are issues, questions or feedback. Today's generations have witnessed and undergone a number of truly revolutionary changes in their lives, triggered and fueled by technological advances that would have only been dreamed of just a few decades ago. These advancements are now almost taken for granted, as part of our daily personal and professional lives.

Our faces are glued to our phones and we can't help from swiping our grimy little fingers across some app that will deliver a pizza straight to our face in under 30 minutes. That's what modern customer experiences are all about: ease, low friction and convenience.

With access to almost everything at literally your fingertips, it is important to keep in mind that every organization has a myriad of routes that directly or indirectly interact with customers. It could be your website, Facebook page, LinkedIn, LiveChat, email, support hotline - the options are endless. What is key in keeping up with the modern world of customer experience is making sure all those dots connect.

Many of you reading this book are using a Customer Relationship Manager (CRM) tool on a daily basis and it's important that all areas of the business understand the power of these types of resources. A well-optimized CRM would record how a prospective customer found your company or offerings (marketing), would support documentation of communication and purchased services (sales), would log customer use and issues (support) and highlight customer ideas and feedback (product). Whether you're using Salesforce, Hubspot, Freshworks, Intercom, Zendesk or some other CRM tool – you already know how important it is to have critical customer information available, especially when things go south with an important customer or key account. It's up to you as your company's ambassador to sort these elements out to best increase your chances for success.

Tools: Every company and customer has their own preferred methods of communication. It's really important to make sure that you know what your customer's preferred methods are so that you can best serve them in future interactions. Always think at scale!

There are still many industries that have not yet seen the type of CX revolution within their corporate and operational practices. Let's take the cable industry for example:

> *A customer calls a 800-number, listens to a list of numerical options in a robot-tone and typically ends up screaming "Operator! Operator!" or pounding on "0" until a human-voice is on the other end. And if this isn't your first time calling, most likely it'll be treated as if it was i.e. starting the complaint from scratch!*

We all have those examples of antiquated policies or processes from a company or service provider that literally makes us want to scream. Don't be *that* company!

Companies that have chosen not to adopt the newer methods of communication continue to see the demand from customers to talk on the phone, expecting a prompt response from a living human. When many of us think of traditional customer experience and service operations, we tend to imagine a massive call center in large cities such as Phoenix, AZ or Nashville, TN or even Buffalo, NY (The Collections Capital of the North East!). We envision pods of people talking through headsets, flickering computer monitors, a constant echo of fingers hastily typing on keyboards.

Team: Did you know that more than 10 million Americans are working in the space that revolves around CX, sales and customer service each and every day?

Often times, these call centers are limited to their own CRM and cannot see the full picture of customer interaction that may have taken place. Here's an example:

> *Bobby just moved to a new neighborhood and needs to set up his internet service. He searches 'internet and {zip code}' and several options pop-up. He clicks on the first website link to find several package options. Bobby then references the Nextdoor app to see if the range is good in the neighborhood. An ad pops up with a discount code within Nextdoor, but when he tries it on the website it gives him an error. He calls the 800-number listed and after a series of failed attempts, he connects with a live-human. Unfortunately since the code was generated from a marketing ad, the customer support representative cannot reference that code to provide the discount and routes him to the Nextdoor app to purchase the service.*

First, I am exhausted just writing that. Second, we have all experienced these merry-go-round situations, which are a reflection of an organization that looks at process as an afterthought.

Process: When designing your business' overall customer journey, remove as much friction as possible - something that might seem minor to you may enhance the perception of your product or business offering for the customer.

With that being said, there can be a balance. Some of the most successful enterprises have demonstrated the incredible power that lies within a personalized customer experience that can be created and replicated within each interaction and transaction.

Take Amazon for example, if you had told someone ten plus years ago that the new normal would be giving an online company all of your money before you ever had a chance to try, touch, or sense the products that you were adding to your shopping cart, people would have thought you were crazy!

Now today millions of Amazon Prime members are regularly stuffing their carts full of crap nearly every day and trusting that one day or a few days later its going to show up on their doorstep ready to be worn, used, inflated, or gifted to a family member or loved one. This company has changed the way that we as consumers think about modern day shopping experiences. When was the last time you went to your local shopping mall? Have you noticed how empty the parking lots have become? Or how there's not nearly the same number of tenants as there was back in the day? Amazon figured out how to scale this entire experience online and make things easier and more convenient for their customers and it's a huge reason why they've become one of the most powerful companies on the planet!

And to be successful at this, the methodology must be powered and sustained by a cultural foundation that permeates the entire organization from the ground up. The founders, C-suite, managers, front-line employees and even recent hires should treat this rule like the company's life depends on it!

Take Zappos for example, the king of online shoe retailers. Zappos has entrenched the power and importance of building a sustainable positive customer experience throughout their employee and customer base over the past 20 years. They are continuously recognized as leaders in the space of taking great care of their customers and doing whatever is necessary to make things right with their customers when there is a breakdown.

Tony Hsieh has long been touted as one of the key CEOs to empower his team to do whatever it takes to keep improving not only their customer experience but their offerings itself. For example, a number of new initiatives within the Zappos Family of Companies comes directly from Zappos' employees having candid, real conversations with their customers about how things could be even better in the future -- and if you look at some of the things that they are doing each day you can see that there's real power behind this approach!

We've identified technology and culture as strong drivers of the modern customer experience, but we haven't addressed data and analytics. An organization can only be successful if proven by progress and experience that simplify the innumerable complexities and challenges that, like it or not, are a typical component of every business' daily operation - in short, nothing is set in stone, use feedback as a resource to drive change.

There's tons of companies out there that do an incredible job with collecting, assessing and responding to customer feedback. We've all received the survey emails from major airline companies after a recent travel experience. The surveys from Delta, American Airlines, Southwest, etc. all look and read pretty similar. They ask us about our travel experiences, wait times within the terminals, they ask for our feedback about their actual airplanes and the gadgets within them (or lack thereof of its an older airplane). The idea here is that they can collect a ton of usable feedback and data around areas that are ripe for improvement. Plus they can clearly see the major areas that they are doing a great job and customers seem to think and score them well on.

All of this customer feedback funnels directly into the teams who focus on continuous improvement (CI) and gets managed up the executive chain to the leadership team responsible for managing and leading the company on the day to day.

With the $62 billion elephant in the room, you can imagine why modern global companies are narrowing their focus on refining and optimizing their customer experience and service efforts.Yet the reality is, not enough companies - specifically small, growth-based businesses - do enough to make collecting customer feedback as a core focus area to build a loyal customer base early on.

Without thoughtfully crafted customer experience, service and loyalty frameworks in place, many companies in today's world wouldn't last very long. As a business owner, you're fighting against the likes of Amazon, Uber, Google, Facebook and others who regularly examine and evaluate their overall customer engagement. The wealth of data these companies have at their fingertips to curate their customer journeys are second to none. Another reason why small business owners and executives must strive to be more innovative and creative than the next when developing memorable customer interactions that will result in brand loyalty.

Process: As a small business owner, you have more agility to make changes to your services and offerings than large enterprises like Google and Facebook. Take advantage of that! How can you differentiate or distance yourselves from the competition when it comes to learning more about every one of your customers?

The constant scoping for customer information and feedback is critical for any business to succeed. It will help identify where a business will be most poised for success as it relates to the development and construction of teams, systems, tools and processes. It's no wonder that Google, Apple, Airbnb, and WeWork are sited as some of the world's leading companies given their drive for customer success is similar to a sports bookie who sets the big game spread to make the maximum return on their investments!

On the same feedback thread, social media is now an integral part of a company's overall CX approach. You may be hearing the buzzword "omnichannel" thrown out more recently this approach is emerging as a burgeoning subject matter across businesses in NYC and San Francisco and other technology hotbeds.

Process: Omnichannel -- also spelled omni-channel -- is a multichannel approach to sales that seeks to provide customers with a seamless shopping experience, whether they're shopping online from a desktop or mobile device, by telephone, or in a brick-and-mortar store.

A business that's focused on having an omnichannel customer communications strategy has the best chance of winning in today's customer driven markets. It relates to the way that your business makes itself available to communicate with its customers for specific interactions. In short, if you make it easy for the customer to connect with you and get the information they need, it will have a direct return on investment (ROI) as customers always come back to the places that make it the most seamless.

Quick exercise: Does your business make it easy for your customers to connect with you? What are the different mediums (i.e. phone, email, Instagram, Facebook, LiveChat, etc.)? Do all correspondences track back to one place? How do you get alerted if a customer reaches out? How do you determine who follows up from the different channels?

For most startup and growth-focused companies, sales, marketing, customer experience and service design all fall under the same umbrella: Revenue. Personalization creates the optimal customer experience regardless of your business type or size. Holistic customer experience is becoming a top priority for many business owners as it's always easier to keep and retain the customers that you already have, than to go out and pay money to find brand new ones.

By taking the time to connect the dots inside of your own company's customer journey map you will find all kinds of financial levers and opportunities for increasing your bottom line. It might be by offering a specific service offering sooner rather than later, or giving something up early in the buying process to gain the customer's trust. By thoughtfully curating the customer experience, you will unearth and identify mountains of opportunity for your business and team to pursue.

Within the next 10 years 50% of the U.S. workforce will be involved in the freelance economy (Uber/Lyft, Fiverr, UpWork, Airbnb, TaskRabbit). This type of economy has key similarities within their customer experiences:

- Instant, rapid interactions
- Convenience or low friction
- Simplified ways humans interact and transact
- Fluid customer engagement across all channels (Omnichannel approach)
- Innovative, unique, cutting edge

These companies are setting the bar incredibly high for the rest of us entrepreneurs, regardless of company size, modern consumers are already beginning to view this as the new normal.

Reflection: What is your company doing that is different from how the competition engages with their customers? What does your customer loyalty program look like? Can you remember the last time your business went out of its way to make a customer happy? Did this bring your company additional revenue in the near future from that positive exchange? What other focus areas can you insert in your daily customer operations to see this same positive impact across other customers or accounts?

CHAPTER TWO

WTF are The Four CX Pillars™?!

2

WTF are The Four CX Pillars™?!

Before we get into the meat and potatoes, I'd like to offer some context for the readers who are new to the CX game: This is not an easy area or department to work within any company or industry. Working directly with customers is hard. It takes time, nerves, and oftentimes wit to quickly make decisions that can make your customers have an incredible experience with your business.

I feel it's important to disclose because you are going to eat loads of bullshit (BS) along the journey of building your business. I've eaten tons of BS over the years - more BS than you can possibly believe at every level and every role throughout my career. In some bizarre way, those bowls of BS made me who I am today.

It's the tough customer scenarios that help to thicken your skin, become more malleable and build your customer-focused arsenal! So with that said, get ready to eat bowls and bowls of crap folks! If you want to get to the top of the "customer" mountain, you need to get ready to climb many boulders of all different shapes and sizes. You may need to try different approaches, you may barn-door every once and awhile or come up against a choss - but enjoy the climb because this will set you apart from 99% of businesses today.

With that all said, developing and honing in on The Four CX Pillars™ did not happen overnight. It took more than 10 years of working inside of multiple venture-backed companies across a variety of industries to establish these Pillars. Outside of my self-driven passion for working directly with customers, I also had the good fortune of working with some of the most amazing, dedicated, hard-working, and empathetic humans that one could encounter. And I'm incredibly grateful for the wisdom those folks have bestowed upon me during my personal journey, this includes work related and personal connections along the way.

After recognizing successful trends and common focus points with my executive leadership teams, I sought out to create a fresh, easy way for business owners and executives to think about what matters the most when growing or scaling their business: the customer. It was time to share this knowledge and help other organizations grow through the power of customer experience by optimizing and investing in The Four CX Pillars™. CXChronicles was born.

By taking the time to think about how you can use The Four CX Pillars™ framework to shape and hone your team for success, you will already be ahead of your competition. Better yet, you will already be completely entrenched in the school of thought around being a customer-focused business leader. This is a customer experience manager playbook for success.

So, what are these damn Pillars?! **Team, Tools, Process and Feedback**

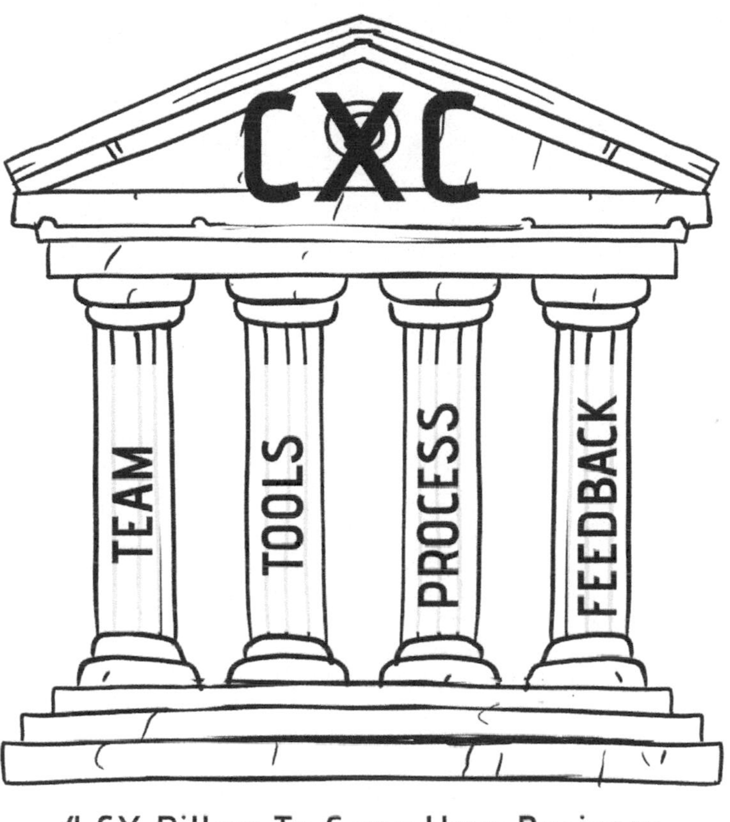

The trends that kept surfacing in my CX journey always seemed to fall into one of these four buckets above. However, I soon realized these weren't buckets - buckets are plastic, cheap, and $5 from a Dollar store. These four focus areas that were far more important, more regal. They were pillars. Big, beautiful, white, Carrara marble Roman-style pillars. The type of pillars that could act as the foundation for a beautiful, brand new, colosseum or state of the art stadium!

The Four CX Pillars™ provide areas of impact regardless of what your business or industry type is. In the next chapters of this book, we will explore each Pillar and identify and highlight the extremely valuable methodology for shaping your business for the better!

CHAPTER THREE

Pillar One - Team

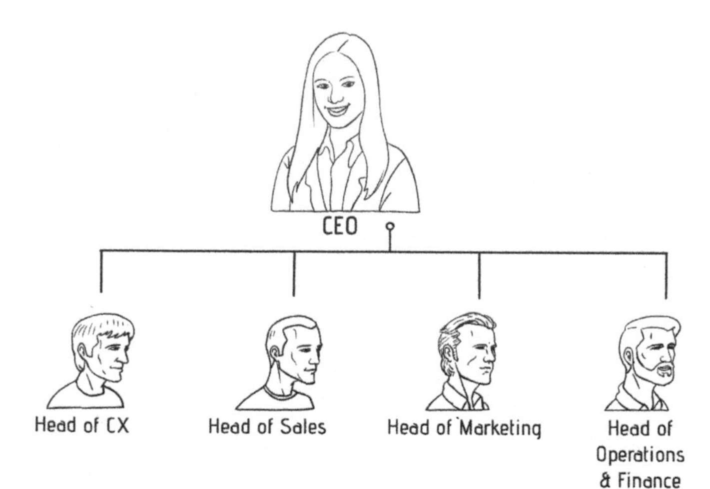

3

Pillar One - Team

The first and arguably the most important of The Four CX Pillars™: **Team.**

When we speak with business leaders on The CXChronicles Podcast, we ask them: "Which of The Four CX Pillars™ do you spend most of your time thinking about?"

The answer is almost always answered the same way: how without a strong, dedicated, well-functioning TEAM all of the other CX Pillars are nearly impossible to manage.

As Abdullah Khan, Head of Customer Experience at FuboTV said in Episode 27 of the CXCP, "Without a strong team in place, the other Pillars will all resemble that of a wobbly chair!"

For example, a company that has a CEO, COO, CTO and a suite of directors and managers who know how to hire, train, manage, and support their growing team and organization is in a much better position than the small restaurant owner who has to think about the kitchen staff, customer base, food and liquor distributors and day-to-day management.

Your team is so important at any stage of any business. Without a solid team organized and loaded top to bottom with the right types of talent, all of the other CX Pillars are compromised or weak. Your Team is and will always be the primary engineers, technicians and servicers of The Four CX Pillars™ therefore, it is critical that you spend time thinking deeply about how you want to craft, shape, and pitch the most important CX Pillar in your company!

Reflection: Think about the last time you were a part of a team that you knew was special: maybe it was at a previous company, a sports team, or even a volunteer organization. Did it feel special because of the overall mission? Was it memorable because every person brought a different value? Or was it because of a certain leader who would always seem to crank up the troops for battle?

It is imperative for customer-focused business leaders to remain maniacal about the importance of teamwork, culture, and creating an environment of accountability, authority and autonomy! This focus alone ensures that you are setting a strong foundation for a cohesive, connected and highly communicative team!

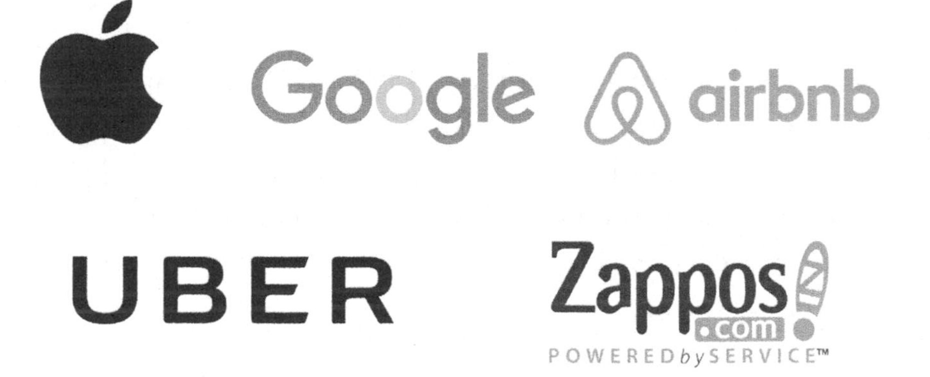

Companies that Have Done it Right

Sure, startup companies have the advantage of being agile and ever changing but there are large, established organizations that pretty much got it right from the beginning. These companies did a great job focusing on their customers and building their businesses completely dedicated to the constant evolution and investment in The Four CX Pillars™. Here are a few that come to mind:

Zappos.com

Zappos: I had the pleasure of touring the Zappos campus in Las Vegas and meeting some of their team members - the "customer" and their "experience" are evidently drivers of all business decisions. Zappos has proven that focusing on establishing a culture built around customers, service and the employee is the best way!

Uber

Uber: This ride-hailing app has become a household name and revolutionized the car industry. It wasn't too long ago that the thought of letting your teenager in a stranger's car was terrifying! Today, that's how we get little Johnny to soccer practice. Uber changed the way that transportation works across the planet all within its clients hands.

Airbnb: This hospitality app took travelling to another level and allowed its clients to experience the world in the eyes of locals. Not to mention, got rid of the antiquated check-in process at hotels.

Apple: From the box it's wrapped in to the way you get started using your new Apple product, this UX god of a company has constantly optimized every touchpoint in a customer journey, while using all the customer's senses.

Google: Once a website, now a verb and personal and professional life manager for many. Google's suite of offerings has become a preferred method of email, calendar, map directions, document sharing, chatting, and the list goes on. These offerings are proof that their success comes from listening to what the customers want and need.

amazon

Amazon: Despite what you may think about the company's leadership or culture, it has transformed the mundane task of shopping to keep up with the fast-paced, distracting world we live in. And with same-day shipping?!

WeWork: If you've never had the privilege of stepping into a WeWork space, they're typically…dope. This company has systematically changed the way that modern real estate and development work across the planet with a nice helping sprinkle of hospitality on top. At the same time don't forget how quickly these rocketship companies can encounter turbulence or even disaster along the way!

Teams within Startups

Being a part of a startup team is a unique situation, especially while managing rapid growth within large customer portfolios. The frequency of change and daily course correction is not for everyone and it takes a certain type of level-headed maniac to truly appreciate what goes into building these companies from the ground up. I am one of those maniacs.

Startup teams are often quickly assembled and team members wear an array of hats in the early days. It is a common practice for start-ups to hire people to "solve problems" instead of finding a long-lasting, scalable solution - I guess it can make sense when you don't know if the lights will be on in a year.

With that being said, the lack of planning for the future can create massive friction with customers. In the heat of the customer-dissatisfaction moment, we will do anything to make our customers happy. But be careful folks, this can be hard to back out later on down the road!

Team Structures

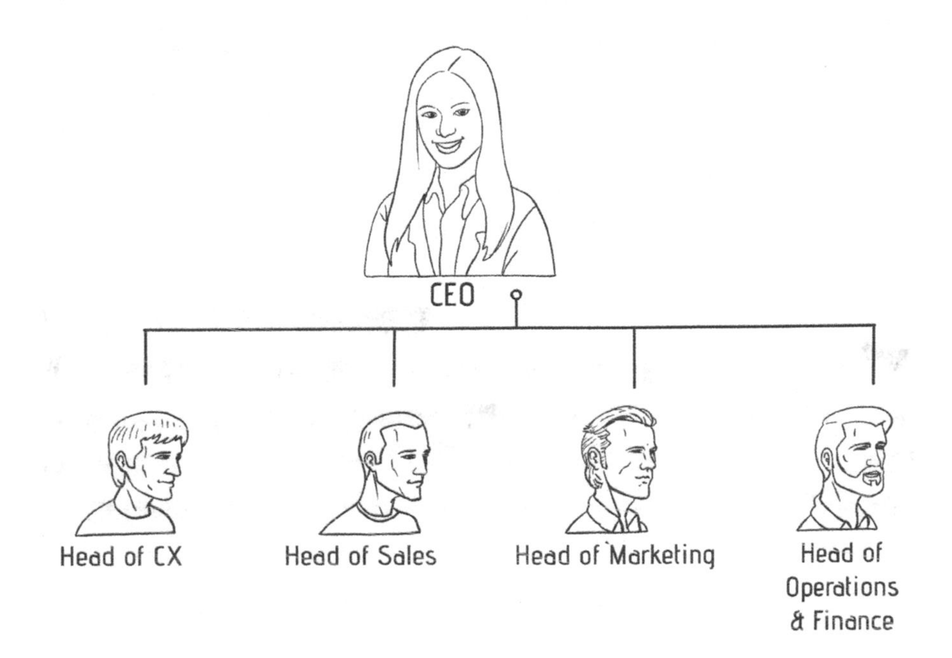

A sound, high-performing CX team needs to understand what their positions and responsibilities are in keeping their customers happy. What is each team member's specific focus area? What CX channels are the monitoring? What does the decision-making tree look like? How do they work with the rest of the business? There's constantly changes happening within any growth focused company - it's important to have someone keeping an eye on all of the inbound/outbound traffic as you grow your business!

Reflection: What would an air traffic controller be without a clear understanding of issue landing and takeoff protocols, flight patterns, and weather warnings? Would you trust an airport without properly trained air traffic team? Probably not...

Similar to how you think about your customer journey map, think about your new hire journey map on this team. In addition to thinking full picture about the role, it is ideal to have alignment within the entire organization on how CX interacts and supports with the different departments. Similar to the holistic customer approach if you can have foresight of how all teams will work together, you have the power to build one indestructible power team!

Quick Exercise: Take the time to envision your organizational chart. It is important to not focus only on who reports to whom, but also include these additional focus areas:

- The company's mission and strategic vision
- Each role, responsibilities and direction
- Customer interactions
- Agility and flexibility
- Company culture

This will allow you to truly build a holistic team and dominate your industry!

How do I Build a Great Team?

So how does one get started with finding the best possible talent for your business? First, think about your business today.

Reflection: Who is part of your team? How does each team member work together? What are the strengths and weaknesses of the business? What are the gaps in the business operations? What tools and resources do you use? What makes your business different from its competitors? What is needed to take the business to the next level?

I can't emphasize this enough, regardless of your business and industry type: people are key in shaping any successful enterprise. Before you even advertise an open opportunity, it is important to think about the full scope of the "team building process":

1. Recruitment: Attract the potential crew to manage the ship
2. Interviewing: Narrow down the elite members who get to board
3. Onboarding & Training: Show them how the damn ship works, mate!
4. Daily Management: Leave port and heading to sea
5. Goal Setting & Performance Metrics: What is our destination today, tomorrow, this year, and what's next? Are you on target to get there before the storm?
6. Career Trajectory and Compensation Planning: From Deckhand to Captain

Recruitment

Recruitment isn't just throwing up free job postings on Indeed and hoping for the best (I should know since my wife worked in the industry for years!). Think of recruitment as dating - you only want to attract prospective mates who you want to potentially spend the rest of your life with. Of course hiring someone doesn't need to be looked at as a life commitment, but you will be spending the majority of your time with your teammates - so it better be someone you enjoy being around!

With that being said, recruitment isn't just what type of person would you like working with, but what skill sets, experience, attitude, work-style, and expertise you need to compliment the team! I suggest collaborating with different areas of the business to share best practices and also look to your external resources - referrals are the best types of prospects! It's a really competitive job market, so be sure to get creative when designing each role.

Interviewing

A prospect hates nothing more than a haphazard, unstructured and repetitive interview process. Be thoughtful of who speaks to prospects, what questions are asked or skills are being assessed, how quickly there is follow-up and next steps are clear.

My wife worked at a recruitment tech company for a number of years and actually, Episode 45 of The CXChronicles Podcast will give you a peek behind the CX scenes of that company. Hearing her sales calls and understanding the problems prospective clients faced, it was clear that many organizations are not thoughtful about their hiring process.

As you are defining the key skills and responsibilities needed for your role in the Recruitment process, be mindful of how to assess those skills in the interview process. Here are some assessment avenues I've found successful:

- Email Sampling: Present a problem to your candidate and have them draft an email response to the customer. This will be a great opportunity to test their grammar, creativity and empathy.
- Mock Live-Chat Session: Have a mock chat session teed up for your candidate with a CX team member on the other end. Don't make the questions ultra complex but just test how quickly and

thoughtfully your candidate can respond - keep in mind they are probably not a product expert yet.

- Testing Tools: There are hundreds, not thousands of testing platforms out there to help you assess your candidates skill-level in the space. Here are a few I've personally used: Criteria Corp, Harver, day100, and Plum.
- Problem-Solving Exercises: Take a real-life challenge in your business, assign it to your candidate ahead of time and have them present a solution to the interview panel. Keep the structure open to allow your candidates to be creative. This is a great opportunity to 'try it before you buy it' and vice versa.

In addition to testing skills appropriately, it is vital you have different employees from different areas of the business as interviewers. Just because someone is interviewing for the CX team, does not mean they will only interact with the CX team - CX is the glue to all the business lines and you should interview for that! This will also allow for a fairer decision-making process after the interviews - the viewpoints will be more well-rounded and not favored to one area of the business.

Onboarding

Team: Did you know about 20% of employees leave within their first 45 days of employment? (Source: Forbes)

You've found your new teammates, now what? Sure, it is important to have your new hires meet the people team and get familiar with the company's policies and resources, but how do they hit the ground running?

Onboarding is critical for setting up your new teammates for future success. When someone joins an organization, it's vital they are provided with proper training and guidance prior to launching into their new role - no matter if they are seasoned vet or novice in the industry. With that said, there is always a grace period in learning a business, introducing yourself to the team, and familiarizing yourself with the customers and processes that drive the company on the day-to-day.

Well one of the simplest resources to develop is a living playbook - this could be a working GoogleDoc, PowerPoint presentations, spiral-bound printouts, or even banners on the wall.

Successful teams across sports, business, politics and entertainment have a constantly evolving document that everyone on the team can refer back to.

In every business I've worked at and every client CXChronicles has worked with, the first item on the agenda is to build a living playbook. Often times, the playbook exercise will even identify gaps in the team, process, workflows, and resources.

Living playbooks or Standard Operating Procedures (SOP) are critical to enforcing alignment within your teams and the rules of engagement for how your business interacts with and for your customers. It should provide the day-to-day direction, definitions of tasks and responsibilities, location of resources, and reporting lines by roles and teams to carry the greater mission forward. Here's an example of what a living playbook table of contents (specific to CX teams) might look like:

1. Company Mission & Core Values
2. Organizational Chart, Team Structure & Reporting Lines
3. Role-by-Role Descriptions (a.ka. Responsibility)
4. Team Process & Workflows (a.k.a. Accountability)
5. Issue Resolution & Escalation Management (a.k.a. Authority)
6. Toolkit & Additional Resources
7. Cheat Sheet: Talk tracks and templates for managing customer issues
8. Case Studies: Share customer success stories!
9. Live Updates: Working area for ideas, questions, comments, version update notes, etc.

The development of these playbooks don't happen overnight - I would advise assigning this to a taskforce of your best players in the game to collaborate and build this together. In addition, demand executive buy-in to ensure the entire business is supporting the project and adopting these across all teams. This should never be a one-person job! And get creative, make it fun, and use modern tools that gain and capture people's attention.

If you don't have a playbook in place and you're still hiring like crazy, shadowing has been a long-standing option for onboarding new hires. Most people learn by doing and shadowing does prove effective from that perspective.

One onboarding that always impressed me was the process at Danny Meyer's Eleven Madison Park in New York City (Michelin 3-star restaurant). It was a common practice for EMP servers to spend one-year shadowing a seasoned employee before ever speaking with a customer. The rationale being there is so much to learn about the world-class "EMP Way" that it was a risk to have someone engage with a customer before they are ready. How does your organization support ramping new employees? How do you know they are ready to engage with your customers? Is there oversight along the way - if not, should there be?

A Western New York family-owned business that consistently ends up on the Fortune magazine "Best Companies to Work For" is Wegmans. These grocery stores not only have high-quality inventory, but their employees are top-notch!

Outside of their delicious prepared-food bar, Wegman's is also known for investing time, money and energy in training and on-boarding their employees. On Wegmans website, they state: "To our CUSTOMERS and our PEOPLE we pledge continuous improvement, and we make the commitment: **Every day you get our best."** Their method is simple, if we focus on our people - internal and external - we will have a big, successful business.

When designing your onboarding process, ensure there are clearly defined tasks, responsibilities and check-ins throughout this process. Also, this experience should be interactive and involve a mix of written content, visual content, and activities centered around your customers & business processes to get new teammates up to speed. We will get into this more in Chapter 5 through shared learning and tribal knowledge - so stay tuned!

Training

If your company isn't taking the time to think about its training efforts to ensure that each team, department, role has clear performance metrics, you are probably struggling to tread water.

One of the first places you can start to improve the overall customer experience in your company is the training investment you make in your staff. Let's start with some basic concepts around team training best practices and fundamentals:

1. Pre-season Training: Even world championship sports teams start their seasons with spring or summer training to get ready for their upcoming season launch.
2. Continued Training: No matter how much experience or knowledge you have, you can always get better and take actions towards improving. Training the "right way to do things" and giving a "playbook for success," should be one of the chief areas you as a leader spend time on, regardless of what the trade or industry.
3. Having a Clear Vision: Team members need clear direction and overall mission early-on. This will engrain the goal for success.
4. Regular Coaching: This is not just one-on-one meetings, this needs to be programmed into the overall chemistry of team building exercises and performance areas.

Daily Management

At this point, we've given our team a playbook that defines their roles and responsibilities so one would hope that it's smooth sailing there. But that's not always the case. I've found that presenting visuals of success (and failures) is a good method of daily motivation. I'm talking about DASHBOARDS!

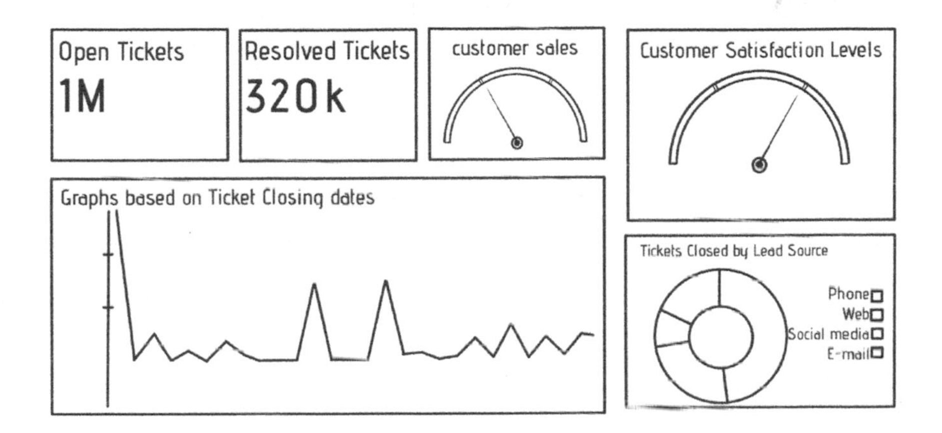

We're going to get into Tools a little later in this book, but I do want to touch on how dashboards impact your daily management of teams. In every business I've worked with, I ensured there was at least a V1 of an active dashboard - whether it was from a working GoogleDoc feed or built within a CRM. This resource gives team managers the opportunity to:

- Keep track of Objectives and Key Results (OKRs) that help steer toward a company's goals
- Define daily goals and Key Performance Indicators (KPIs)
- Uncover areas for improvement

- Identify team successes - it can't always be about the bad stuff, folks
- Spotlight top performers and factors of their success
- Diagnose under performers and opportunities for coaching or performance plans
- Share CX performance with executive team
- Create the "heartbeat of the customer" or the "customer health score" to quantify your customer portfolio

And once you have these data points available, they should be somewhere for everyone in the business to see. As a CX team, you should be proud of your wins and if there aren't enough, then use the dashboard as an opportunity to drive morale in the right direction!

Speaking of morale, in Episode 16 of The CXChronicles Podcast, Mac Hansen, former Head of Customer Experience at a very large software company based out of Seattle - nudge nudge, wink wink - reflected there were two quotes that stuck with him during his CX leadership journey:

> *Every business leader needs to focus on cultivating culture before diving down the "data" rabbit hole.*

> *If you celebrate people regularly, they will stay engaged.*

In my career, I've had the privilege of working with a number of amazing startup teams in New York City. There was a number of team-building activities that we would always lean on during times of growth, expansion, or the general hardships that come along with being a part of the team that is building, scaling and leading a startup or growth-based business. Some of my favorite team-building activities included:

- Local Watering Hole Gatherings: Not to say that alcohol makes everything better but for some folks enjoy a nice refreshing cocktail after a long day of customer escalations.
- Intramurals Sport Teams: For people and companies that would rather not promote drinking activities, form a softball, basketball, soccer, kickball or broomball league to get your team together for healthy activities outside of the office.
- Team Off-Site Meetings: Getting your team out of the routine office space and into a new, open venue can inspire ideas and solutions of how to get smarter, faster, and better!
- Weekly Team Meetings: It is imperative you have a rhythm of assembling your role-based teams. Take this opportunity to facilitate "show and tells" - have different team members share something they learned that week with the rest of the team, and rotate. Most people learn from seeing, then doing. By hearing stories from the field, you can improve your game and better understand the challenges in front of you.
- Cross-Functional Meetings: Silos can be the death of a seemingly successful business! Make sure there is a cadence for different departments to connect, share and collaborate ideas.
- Quarterly Fun Days: Once every quarter, take the entire team (or even better, company) out for random acts of fun! This could be a scavenger hunt around the town, a day at a theme park or a "team olympics" with different field activities. Your team will get a chance to take a mental break from customer escalations and enjoying being together!

When in doubt, do them all!

Goal Setting & Performance Metrics

Once a team is properly trained inside of The Four CX Pillars™ (Team, Tools, Process and Feedback), you can begin to place and manage expectations on specific performance metrics or Key Performance Indicators (KPIs).

KPIs are guiding data points to help steer the focus and energy put into your business. Performance metrics show clear numbers related to projected goals and actual performance areas across different teams, roles or department within a company.

Setting goals is critical for success. Whether you are an individual or a team, goal setting is one of the easiest ways that you can set some basic achievements in front of you that you can aim for. If you were to poll all of the world's best athletes you'd find that setting goals and identifying key milestones within that journey is one of the biggest factors in their success. For example, if benching 300 lbs. 10X is what it's going to take to make or exceed the next level then you need to set goals towards that accomplishment. In business you can't make your first $1 million in sales without your first $1,000.00 - there's goals along the way that will get you up to the top of the mountain.

I mentioned this briefly in our dashboards talk, but it is vital to define KPIs along with your role responsibilities. These will be drivers to your team's success and keep them working hard to achieve, especially if these are sitting on your daily dashboards!

KPIs also function as a great coaching mechanism. If you see a team member is far from reaching their number in a week, a month or a quarter, those KPIs can quickly identify the areas of improvement and offer an opportunity for improvement. Using KPIs to act as a mechanism for sharpening your team's ability to hit goal posts is a good exercise. Folks need some basic direction to be able to effectively line up their sights on a given target.

Take a few minutes to think about what some of the key KPIs are within your business or team. Do they line up accurately to where you want your employees focused? More importantly do they line up to what matters most to your customers?

Career Trajectory

Another huge component of successful team building includes employee feedback and performance reviews. Quarterly and 360 reviews for individuals, teams or departments are always helpful for understanding what you do great and highlighting areas that you need to improve.

Team: A 360 review or 360-degree feedback is a process through which feedback from an employee's subordinates, colleagues, and supervisor(s), as well as a self evaluation by the employee themselves is gathered.

Make sure that everyone participates in these reviews. It helps to build a culture of accountability and feedback from the top of the organization to the bottom. If you're still busy getting your company or team off the ground, then annual reviews are an absolute minimum starting point!

Another team-based practice I've always favored involves gathering the knights (i.e. a representative from every area of the business, but not a team leader) around the table to discuss your customer operations' strengths, weaknesses, opportunities and threats (SWOT).

Process: A SWOT analysis organizes your top strengths, weaknesses, opportunities, and threats into an organized list and is usually presented in a simple two-by-two grid. Even though the knowledge identified is at a high level the SWOT analysis enables you to make more informed decisions and increase your chances of success.

This impactful business analysis can be another way to define the leaders of the pack within your organization and offer your top performers a venue to show off their skills. Here is a quick breakdown of how it works:

1. Identify your company's internal factors (from a high level): Things that you have some control over and can change (i.e. strengths and weaknesses)
2. Identify your external factors (from a high level): Things that are going on outside your company, in the larger market (i.e. opportunities and threats)

3. Match opportunities to your strengths
4. Where possible, convert any threats or weaknesses into strengths or opportunities

When you take the time to do a SWOT analysis, you'll be armed with new ideas and strategies to prioritize the right work to build your business. And as a cherry on the top, you've gathered your top performers to take a stab at leadership responsibilities - I'd say that's a definite plus!

Quick Exercise: Let's do a "speed" SWOT analysis! Here are some questions to ask yourself:

- Strengths: What are you doing today to kill it within your marketplace? What assets do you have in your team, such as knowledge, network, skills, and reputation? What physical assets do you have, such as customers, capital, technology, and assets? What competitive advantages do you have over your competition?
- Weaknesses: Are there things that your business needs to be competitive? What areas in your business lacks moxy? Are there tangible assets that your company needs? These might include things your competitors do better than you, What are the gaps to your team or offerings? What potentially limits your growth and ability to scale?
- Opportunities: What areas of your business or team has the potential to improve? Is your market growing and are there trends that will encourage people to buy more of what you are selling? Are there upcoming events that your company may be

able to take advantage of to grow the business? What do your customers think of you?

- Threats: Do you have potential competitors who may enter your space? Are there market trends that could become a threat? Is there any press or media that can negatively impact your business? Could future developments in technology change how you do business?

Once your SWOT analysis is complete, you're now ready to convert your hard work into real strategy and now you have identified the leaders to take you there. At the end of the day, this exercise is all about producing the strategy to grow your business!

CHAPTER FOUR

Pillar Two - Tools

4

Pillar Two - Tools

We now know that investing in the right teammates early-on will ensure a strong foundation for your business. When it's time to scale, it is common that tools are the next resource to be invested in.

There's an old saying: Give me six hours to chop down a tree and I will spend the first four sharpening the axe. In reality I've only picked up an axe a handful of times, but do I know that properly dedicating time in the maintenance of your tools will always result in success. In this chapter, we will take a deeper dive into the tools and resources key to every badass CX team!

Today companies are expanding their toolkits faster than ever before, thanks to the continuous and rapid development of new technology. Here are some of the basic tools in a CX team's arsenal:

- Email: This is your inbound/outbound way of messaging customers and your team each and every day - and sometimes small businesses' only line of defense in the early days.
- Phone: Whether these are individual desk lines or an auto-dialer solution, 70% of consumers still want to talk with a human.
- Live Chat: Don't drive your customers away from your website, answer their questions right where they have them.

- Social Media: Facebook, Instagram, Twitter, Snapchat and LinkedIn have all taken over the way that we share updates and information with our prospects and customers. Being present across all of these social channels is critical in today's world.
- Ticketing Management System: Once your business gets to a certain size you need to have a tool like Zendesk, Intercom or Freshdesk to help you keep all of your customer interactions or to-do's aligned.
- Customer Relationship Management (CRM) solution: Vital resource to keeping all of your customer (and prospective customers) interactions centralized.
- Internal Messaging Services: Slack, Chatter, Google Chat have all become common venues for companies to engage internally.

There a number of new tools and solutions out there that make it simple and easy for your team to begin managing all of the omni-channel customer interactions your business sees each day.

Within each of those tools are different variations - not all screwdrivers are the same right? Let's start with my personal favorite customer experience weapon - phones.

Phones

There are three common business telephone systems that many of you will encounter along your customer experience journeys; Key System Units (KSU), Private Branch Exchange (PBX), Voice Over Internet Protocol (VOIP) and Interactive Voice Response (IVR) systems.

KSU (Key System Units) are typically suitable for small businesses with 40 employees or less. This system uses a central switching device to manually determine optimal phone line selection. KSU can act as a great solution for teams that are not rapidly growing, but if you're planning on blitzscaling in the future then you might want to consider other options.

Process: Common in the startup world, "blitzscaling" is a specific set of practices for igniting and managing accelerated growth. It prioritizes speed over efficiency in an environment of ambiguity, and allows a company to go from "startup" to "scaleup" at a rapid pace that captures the attention of the market. To learn more, check out *Blitzscaling* by Reid Hoffman and Chris Yeh.

PBX (Private Branch Exchange) tends to be more advanced than the KSU systems. It uses programmable switching devices allowing for automatic routing of specific calls. This system will easily manage 40+ employees and allows for expanded capabilities if your company or team already has clean, clear dedicated teams for specific customer matters.

VOIP (Voice Over Internet Protocol) is the latest offering in this space and most advanced system by far. It works with the use of the internet and computer and allows customers and agents to speak with each other from almost anywhere in the world. However, this tends to be the most costly system for your business, as it relates to the number of employees that you have on your front lines each and every day. Most VOIP systems can be hosted, which provides less installation and maintenance involved for your company and team.

And lastly, there's the Interactive Voice Response (IVR) systems, which allows a computer to interact with customers through the use of voice and dual-tone multi-frequency (DTMF) tones input via a keypad, also known as "touch tone" which is a registered trademark of AT&T. IVR systems can respond with pre-recorded or dynamically generated audio to further direct users on how to proceed. They are sized to handle large call volumes and are used for outbound calling.

Emails

When it comes to Email, there are three popular resources: Outlook, Google and Apple.

Founded in 1996 as Hotmail and running as a market leader until 2012, Microsoft Outlook is a trusted email provider for most Fortune 500 companies. Most of us started our computer acumen using Microsoft products and today, there is still the debate around Google vs. Outlook.

Google has taken over the business world with its G Suite offerings and has become very common among startup and growth-focused businesses. Whether its Gmail, GCalendars, GSheets, or GDecks to share around updates Google has made it very easy - given the collaborative nature of its products - and affordable to create and share work across the business, and even with your customers.

Apple's iCloud is a cloud storage and computing service with more than 850 million users using the service in 2018. iCloud enables users to store data such as photos, videos, and documents on remote servers for download or sharing with other users. iCloud also allows users to backup their files and work for later download and usage. For Mac-run businesses, this tends to be a popular option.

Live Chat

The ability to chat directly with prospects and customers can be a game changer in today's competitive market. Some companies have been at this for years now and others are just beginning to see the benefits of how live-chat can pull potential customers through the pipeline or quickly and easily solve a customer inquiry without having to jump through the hoops of a telephone call.

Sourced from The Daily Egg, 2019.

- 29% of consumers have talked with their friends about a positive live-chat experience
- 38% of consumers are more inclined to buy from brands that have live-chat available
- 51% of consumers are more likely to stay with a brand that offers live-chat assistance

Some of the leading live chat software providers include:

- Zendesk Chat is a great option for businesses already using Zendesk for parts of their customer experience and service. The platform is highly flexible and you can create specific customer messages or choose from a bank of templated options. There's also loads of built-in analyticS to help understand how your team is stacking up on the live-chat front, including chat logs. They offer an agent-based pricing model, but is a simple add-on feature for existing customers.
- Intercom is another solution that offers products focused on customer messaging, marketing and customer service all-in-one

platform. Intercom also boasts that they are leading the way in using AI & machine learning to optimize your customer experience over time. Intercom can help users with a variety of tasks including; capturing and converting leads, onboarding and engaging customers, retaining and supporting customers, and even providing self-help options for customers.

- Olark claims to be "the world's simplest live chat option out there." One of the biggest pros for this tool is that all of your customer chat libraries are completely searchable so finding keywords is a breeze. The platform also integrates easily with Salesforce, Hubspot, Google, and MailChimp. If you're looking for a simple straightforward solution, this might be your ticket - no pun intended!
- Pure Chat is the only offering on this list that is completely FREE to users! That alone is a major differentiator and can allow you to get a feel for what live chat can do for your business. Pure Chat focuses on live chat only, you can save and store live chat transcripts and get a sense for if this tool will help your business grow.

Social Media

Social media is a vital tool in curating and managing your business' client communications and customer interactions. Leveraging these social tools will help ensure your business is out there and able to be searched by potential customers, many new customers will search for your brand via one of these mediums before finding your company website or storefront.

Focus on the major players - Facebook, Instagram, Twitter, LinkedIn, Google and Apple - when building out your online social media toolkit. Plus, this is an easy way to expand the different ways that you can communicate with your customers and continue to optimize your specific omni-channel customer approach into the future.

- Facebook - It's not often you come across who hasn't used Facebook, whether to keep in touch with old friends, follow news or media updates, engage in social communities or find new companies or brands, Facebook has become standard for business' online presence. For many businesses it may be the primary avenue for customers to communicate with you about your product or service offerings. It's super common for customers today to start their outreach directly on one of these social channels. There's nearly 2.5 billion active users within this network as of 2019.
- Instagram - One of my personal favorites is Instagram as it acts as a modern magazine. By way of adding or sourcing a variety of accounts to follow, you begin to stitch together a stream of captivating visual and audio content to draw from on a regular basis. For companies out there focused on producing an incredible customer experience this channel acts as an incredible way to tell your brand's story by way of photos, videos, sounds, etc. It also serves as another medium for your customers and employees to communicate, comment, like or share all of the amazing things your company is doing day in and day out! Today, there are more than one billion users using IG, with 71% of them under the age of 35 years old.
- Twitter - Founded in 2006, Twitter has become incredibly common resource for news and immediate updates. Even leaders of the free world are using this tool to get their messages out there in the public. Today, there are more than 330 million

daily users of Twitter with nearly 12 million downloads occurring in the Q1 of 2019 alone! In short, if you need to cast a wide outreach net and quickly, Twitter is a powerful resource.

- LinkedIn - This leading social platform for professionals is not only an avenue for people to publicize their evolving resumes but also your Holy Grail for recruiting and sourcing new talent and take your business to the next level. Today, there are more than 30 million daily users and 92% of Fortune 500 companies use LinkedIn to highlight their talent.
- Google Reviews - When searching for the best dim sum restaurant in a neighboring town, it has become very common for dinner-goers to search Google Reviews to narrow down their choices. Google Reviews provide a tech-savvy way for customers to quickly "gut check" whether or brand or business. It is critical that your company is constantly being reviewed, soliciting reviews and responding. Check out your current Google rating and set goal to move the rating north moving forward!
- Apple Reviews - Similar to Googles, Apple App Store Ratings are one of the first places prospective customers will look to get the quick and dirty on your company on your app. Take the time to provide feedback for these reviews and always ask your customers for input. If they have not had a chance to leave you a review, tell them you will be happy to help them along the way, even if that means hopping on the phone and dictating their response to make it easier for them to post for you. Every positive online review counts folks - this is a form of modern customer currency!

Ticket or Case Management Systems

Once your business starts scaling and growing, what do you do with all the mounting customer inquiries and communications? We could each name an example of a company that is or was overloaded with customer requests or orders - there still might be stacks of order forms and mountains of paperwork in that setting to this day. Today, much of this clutter is organized digitally for future reference or even better - to make analytical sense out of it all.

To help your business keep track of all of the inbound/outbound communications with its customers, you need to decide which tool will house all of this information. Tickets (or cases) helps you with keeping specific customer information organized around questions, inquiries, communications, activities or even troubles during the customer's unique journey with your business.

Tickets help your team create a clean, clear storyline for your customer experience agent to understand their exact customer journey within your business. Tickets help with tagging and identifying key trends or patterns within an organization's day-to-day. By using a CRM, tickets transform into data goldmine to learn more about customer segments, personas, buying behaviors and churn. Here are some commonly used ticketing systems:

- Zendesk: One of the world's leading issue-resolution or ticketing software.
- Freshdesk: One of the easiest, cleanest ways to keep track of customer issues.
- Jira: A trusted classic solution for managing problem tickets for customers or technology issues.

- Intercom: One of the fastest growing solutions that many companies are moving over to.
- Hubspot service: Helping small companies manage their daily customer asks.
- Salesforce Cases: Cases is another form of "tickets" for rapidly growing businesses.

Customer Relationship Management Tool (CRM)

Many of you are already very familiar with some of the main tools out there like Salesforce, Hubspot and Zendesk. These solutions can help your customer-facing teams with their day-to-day customer tasks, but like an iceberg there are is so much below the surface of the water. Once your business gets to a certain size and the volume of communications (emails, phone calls, texts, meetings, etc.) is on the rise, you will likely convert the way you manage your customers issues, communications and information into solutions like the ones below:

- Salesforce: 'The Mafia of CRMs' as CXChronicles Podcast guest Ryan O'Connor likes to joke call it in Episode 34
- Hubspot: A light-weight CRM tool, perfect for small or mid-sized businesses
- freshsales: Part of the freshworks business suite
- Pipedrive: A sales teams version of Trello
- Honorable Mentions: Sugar, Zoho and Base CRM

One of the main reasons you eventually need a CRM tool is to be able to compile all of the valuable information you collect each day from your customers - likes, dislikes, preferences, redflags, concerns, etc. Another is to be able to pull reports on specific areas of your business ripe for analysis. Creating, dissecting and using reporting has become one of the easiest ways to use basic data sets to drive your business into the future, regardless of its size.

Internal Messaging Services

There's a number of ways that your team can communicate internally. As companies experience growth - from ten employees to 100 employees or even 1,000+ - you immediately see how hard it can become to effectively communicate across your business.

It is imperative to find a way to effectively broadcast your morning, afternoon and evening company news.

Reflection: Take a minute to think about your favorite local news provider. How do they organize their daily episodes - global news, regional news, weather, sports and arts? This same rationale can be done inside of your business - take each one of the major areas of your team or departments and begin splitting up the daily, weekly or monthly updates.

For example, Sales will provide updates on big wins and new customers that you're bringing into the business. Operations will highlight the amazing feat your team went through to deliver for your customers and the Product and Technology team will share the exciting new developments to move forward in a systematic fashion, this includes customers and employees. So what are some internal messaging services available today?

- Slack has quickly taken over the internal messaging world with more than 600,000 businesses using their tool every day. There's nearly one billion messages sent per week via Slack and growing. Slack has allowed for employees to spend more time doing the actual work instead of sitting, meeting and wasting time hearing others talking about the work that they will comically never end up doing nor understand how to do in the first place. It's become an incredible time saver and allows for companies to remain tightly knit once they start growing beyond 1,000 employees. It's easy to begin creating specific channels or team views for the right people to be apart of a given discussion or meeting topic.
- Chatter is the tool developed by Salesforce to allow for internal messaging to happen right inside of your CRM. Similar to Slack, Chatter allows you to have conversations with different users inside of your business or team. You are able to like, comment

or post within specific groups or teams inside of your company. Each user has the ability to see these updates in a variety of different ways; emails, desktop chatter app, etc. so you are always in the know for specific tasks or initiatives happening within your business. There's also ample flexibility around searching or adding recommendations around your key focus areas within the business.

- Google Talk (formerly GChat) is an older but great option for team chatting and communication. It's simple and easy-to-use plus allows for easy team dialogue and sharing of project or document updates. This is a great option for any size business to communicate internally by way of chat or video or audio calls, if needed. It's also a super easy way to communicate with your teammates during customer phone calls or meetings. For example: During customer escalation calls, you can coach or manage your team by chatting while speaking to your customer without them ever knowing there's collaboration happening during the activity. Not to mention for smaller, niche businesses this is an incredible way to communicate with your customers. Nothing is more impressive to a potential customer then you popping onto a Google Hangout and chatting with them directly face to face!
- Zendesk Chat is one of a handful of CRMs that also has its own built-in messaging tools which allows for agents to communicate directly with each other during or in between customer interactions. Zendesk Chat allows your team to share ticket information, customer information or issue resolution details inside of their chat solution. This is a great resource for a front-line facing team that shares the inbox or ticket loads and needs to be able to see what their teammates just told the given customer on the last interaction.

Reflection: It's important to spend a couple of minutes each week inside of your team meetings or huddles talking about how your internal messaging tool is working and what you need to do to continue to improve its use and value for serving your customers and employees over time. When's the last time you asked your team about this subject?

By having your team setup with the optimal tools, your team members are much more prepared and ready to scale.Your front-line CX team can begin organically building out the V1 (version 1 aka first prototype) process or workflow that naturally arrives from the day-to-day management of customer communications.

Other Technology

Companies like Twilio and Smooch by Zendesk offer a suite of solutions for companies that prefer to see all customer interactions in one place. These tools can also be connected back to your CRM. Reporting is key for tracking KPIs and managing your team, below are some examples:

- Analytics and reports are the most important focus point for management and leadership. You need to be able to see your performance over a daily, weekly and monthly view to see what's working and what isn't.
- Eventually you'll want to think about establishing SLAs (Service Level Agreements) for your customers, based on what you are seeing inside of your customer reports.

- Ordering and prioritizing your customer problem tickets in a way that allows you to effectively manage your overall customer communications.
- Regular Net Promoter Score (NPS) overview -- how are your customers doing?
- Regular Customer Satisfaction (CSAT) overview -- are your customers happy?
- Regular Product feedback overview -- are you giving your product and development team clean, clear, direct feedback from your customers?

Surround yourselves with technology to improve the chances of your business being able to succeed.

Dashboards

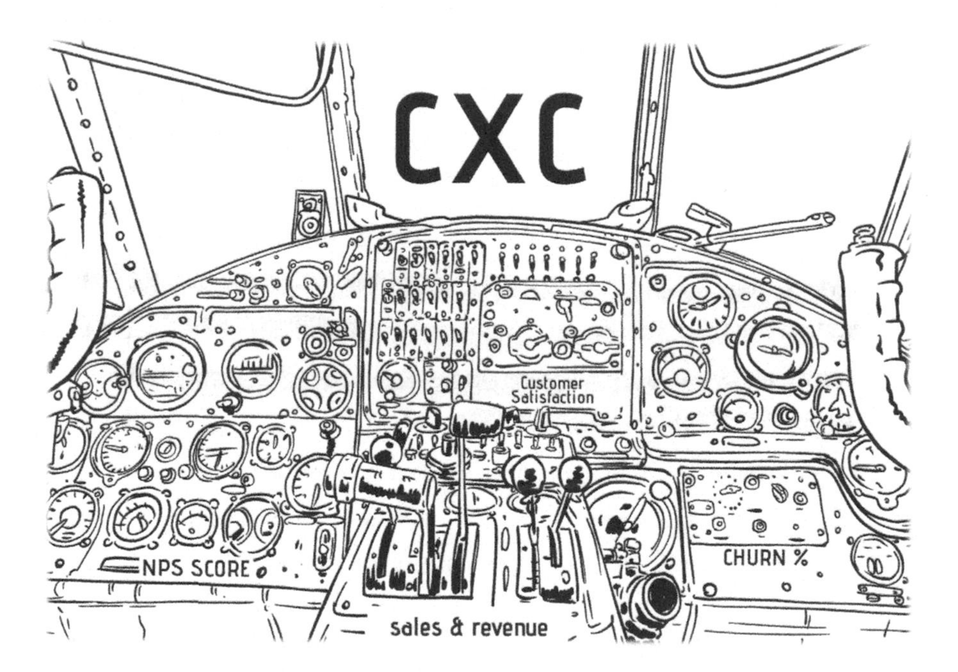

Performance dashboards are another great tool for ensuring that the KPIs and performance metrics that you've set for your team are prioritized and act as a constant reminder for goals.

Dashboards are visual guides to show you how all of your vitals are stacking up on a given day, month or quarter. They might include reports like agent leaderboards, number of activities, issue resolution time, number of tickets/cases completed, etc.

Managing large teams and having full visibility on your performance vitals is critical. If you are not at the point where your company needs full-blown dashboards for your team, any type of visual tools that you can develop will be helpful for your staff and maybe even your customers. You see, well-managed small businesses have whiteboards, chalk boards or even computer monitors set up to help display or highlight things that need to be done on a given shift or within area of the business.

It's amazing what type of results you can achieve by simply increasing your attention, focus and prioritization of a given area within your business. Dashboards are an incredibly powerful tool to get you and your team where you want to go!

CHAPTER FIVE

Pillar Three - Process

5

Pillar Three - Process

'Process' might sound like the most boring thing that we could spend a chapter of our lives reading about, BUT for your business' CX and service they are essential and will be well worth the read, I promise! The companies that prioritize the establishment, documentation, people-management, and ongoing optimization of processes and workflows typically get ahead and beat out their competition. It is essential to the establishment of a cohesive, structured, well-led team of champions. Let's start with the nature development of process: Shared Learning & Tribal Knowledge.

Shared Learning & Tribal Knowledge

I took an anthropology course in "The North Country" about primates and their contribution to the world and one specific bit of "monkey knowledge" that I always remembered was the notion that primates were one of the few animals to display methods of tribal learning. For example, when one primate watched another drink from a river with a reed straw, it would eventually figure out that same newly acquired skill for itself. "Monkey see, monkey do," get it?

This idea is simple and makes perfect sense: shared learning! No matter if you are working in accounting, marketing or product development, there is always something new to share with your fellow co-workers or primates. And it is instinctual for us to want to mimic others as well as share those learnings. So how do we make it useful for our business?

I have seen first-hand how shared learning can work really well for team development and cultural expansion across the business. Here are some examples of how I've seen it be successful:

- Lunch & Learns: Select a subject matter expert (SME) and let him/her run point with your team (or company) to teach something they have mastered. This can be a new way to deal with a particular customer issue, how to make a killer ROI case for a prospective customer or maybe even something completely unrelated to work like new yoga stances. Take turns and create a cadence. It's teambuilding, education, brainstorming and Q/A all mixed all in one. What can be better than that?
- Inter-Departmental Shadowing Exercises: Stop the silos! Welcome folks from different departments to spend time shadowing and learning about other what other areas of the business are doing. This can actually be a great way to spark new ideas and allow Sally in Sales to know what it's like for Amanda in Accounting when the business doesn't get that invoice!
- Local business events: No matter if you're in Silicon Valley, the Big Apple or the Queen City, there are always local business events happening. There are tons of professional organizations that exist to help form connections and business allies across all industries. Encourage your team to attend these events - not only is it great networking but you never know who you will meet (potential new client or new hire) and want opportunities will fall onto your lap!

I mentioned this in Chapter 2 about Tools, but if you can get your "tribal knowledge" down on paper (i.e. playbook or SOP), you're helping set up your business for success and scalability. Each team should have reliable sources of information as their go-to when they have questions, thoughts, concerns and feedback, especially as it relates to their customer communications. These tools were created for a reason folks, they help your team come together and become best prepared to take care of your customers!

Giving your team clarity and visibility around exactly what's going inside of your company and your customers does nothing but make your organization and people stronger and more well-rounded. Pass that knowledge around and make sure you give people the opportunity to always be learning and expanding their own personal curiosities. You never know where or when you'll find your company's next Tom Brady in the sixth round (just make sure he/she isn't a ball-deflating cheater).

Design Thinking

Intentional, well-designed experiences are critical for your customers to have a sound experience with your company's product or service offerings. My favorite imagery of 'what not to do' is a post office line filled with sad-looking prospective customers standing hopefully in line while holding back their internal shrieks of frustration and wiping the drool from their face as they barely shuffle forward. Too much? I didn't think so either -- it always helps me visualize a terribly designed experience when speaking with my clients or teams.

To be perfectly honest, so many companies get this piece wrong when designing their customer experiences. No matter how great your product or service offering is, how involved your team members are - design thinking and user experience is mandatory for getting an edge in today's business world. Having each customer journey step and touchpoint well-versed and ready for your customer makes it easier to increase the chances of those customers coming back, and maybe even bringing their family and friends along with them in the future. Seamless, friction-free experiences get rewarded and create a plethora of promoters - this is what your business needs plenty of to get the fires started!

Process: Design Thinking involves a number of specific processes including; context analysis, problem finding and framing exercises, generating potential ideas around possible solutions, creative thinking or brainstorming, sketching, modeling prototypes as well as testing and evaluating all of the above.

Design thinking is the process of digging deeply into a given problem or user's set of experiences in order to unravel its core design and potential solutions. It has become increasingly popular as more businesses have begun using this method to better understand their customers and present their product or services accordingly. It's also really important to make sure that you have the right brain-trust around the table during specific design thinking exercises. For example, if the problem you are about to begin designing for involves sales, marketing and finance - then be sure to include a stakeholder from each specific area of your business to make sure that all areas are covered.

Thinking through all of the complex layers of a problem or experience and forcing your team to walk through every detail of the process will help you understand the entirety of any situation.

To start, you have to unravel all of the elements of the focus area like an onion. Each team, tool, process and feedback node is like a layer of that onion. As a customer-focused business leader, you are constantly dissecting and analyzing each layer as your business grows. As each layer gets peeled back you begin to learn and identify more and more about the given user and/or experience they are facing. This develops an abundance of opportunity for future optimization.

Design thinking is about understanding your customers several layers deeper than at a transactional level. If you know what makes your customers tick, you are able to design your product or service through those lens. Essentially working backwards to your goals once you understand which elements drives a given experience.

The design thinking exercise can massively improve your business as it forces you to approach your customer, product and service in an entirely different fashion. Here is how it works:

Design Thinking Reflection For Your Business:

1. **Emphasize: Research Your User's Needs** *What are their wants? What are their needs?*

2. Define: State Your Users' Needs and Problems *What barriers are your users up against? What patterns do you observe? What is the big user problem that your team needs to solve?*

3. Ideate: Challenge Assumptions and Create Ideas *What are alternatives to the current state? Are there different angles to approach the problem?*

4. Prototype: Start to Create Solutions *What are the constraints or flaws in this option? Does it need improved or rejected?*

5. Test: Try Your Solutions Out

These designed choices create emotion or response in your customers, whether its negative or positive is a different story. If you are aware of these design queues that make a difference in the satisfaction of your customer, you will be in control of the design elements and increase your chances of keeping those customers coming back! To learn more about design thinking, listen to Episode 56 of CXChronicles with Jeff Gothlef of Lean UX.

Customer Journey Mapping

Customer Journey Mapping (CJM) is an incredibly effective practice for businesses of any size, shape or industry. Similar to design thinking, the customer journey map is taking a look at your company's product or service through the customer's lens, but in a different method. For example, many business owners tend to build their business from the outside in, but building out a CJM forces you to look at how your customers interact with your team and product in the present.

Naturally, a company will design its processes by the immediate needs of its growing volume of customers at that specific point in time. I would be lying if I told you I've never had that happen at a company before, sometimes you just have to put out fires. But when you lay out those fires, ashes and flooded basements out on post-it notes on a conference room wall, it proves your process is quite chaotic. Don't worry, I will explain the post-it notes shortly - stay with me!

The CJM exercise will help bring your team out of the weeds of the day-to-day and surface every interaction they have with your customers. After months and years of performing similar customer experience tasks and activities like phone calls, emails, texts and even customer meetings can become routine and repetitive. Even the best of us want to rip our phone off our desks and whip it against the wall like an animal from time to time. Don't laugh, I know that you've thought about it before. Better yet, some of you have actually done it before with confirmed witnesses haha, you animals! So, how does the Customer Journey Mapping exercise work?

1. Select a group of "CJM Explorers." Make it clear that you are about to embark upon mapping your company's offerings from A to Z, which will require candor, patience and clear communication from all participants.
2. Equip your team with arsenal! (i.e. post-it notes, poster boards, colored markers, tape and plenty of snacks!)
3. Designate a space - whether it's your favorite conference room, a large blank wall or an off-site venue. Keep in mind, you may need this dedicated space for a while, so make sure you won't be kicked out within hours!
4. Outline the parameters as follows:
5. Top Row - Lifecycle Stages: These are all of the unique stages within your specific customer journey for your product or service offerings

a. Awareness: Typically from your marketing efforts, this is when your customer first comes across your business or brand.

b. Consideration: This is when engagement with your potential customer begins - it may be email, phone, or targeting social messaging. It's not just about making contact here, it's about the right kind of contact at the right frequency.

c. Conversion: When your potential customer converts into a real paying customer ready to rock and roll. Don't forget to sell the relationship here, not just the product!

d. Retention: Now that you've gotten your customers' attention and commitment, a proper onboarding will lead to long-term customer success. And in order to retain great customers, a business must offer even greater Support, Adoption programs, Engagement initiatives, and Expansion opportunities.

e. Loyalty: As you begin to create an army of customers who are all promoting your business and very happy with their experiences with your company, you will need to shift your focus towards building out your customer loyalty programs and initiatives.

6. Ascending Rows: Focus Areas

a. Touchpoints: Tangible assets that a potential or existing customer sees when experiencing your company or brand. This includes but is not limited to the website, app, sales assets, social sites and any other medium that might draw in a new potential customer.

b. Challenges: The areas within the CJM that are ripe for improvement. Maybe there's no standard process for where leads and opportunities become familiar with your company or multiple roles are cross-stepping early on in the pipeline?

c. Metrics/KPIs: These are the existing or potential areas within any given CJM that you need to begin measuring, assessing and iterating on a regular basis.

d. Opportunities: When Challenges meet Solutions and from the CJM exercise, there are quickly identified areas for improvement with existing or easy route for change.

7. From here you and/or your team go to work parsing out the details of your business's customer experience journey step-by-step.

   a. To Start, think about the major buckets in the above sections and place them at the top of your whiteboard or working wall; Awareness, Consideration, Conversion, Retention, Loyalty.

   b. On the far left side you need to lay out your major cross areas to populate accordingly, these will include the following; touchpoints, challenges, metrics, & opportunities.

   c. It's most helpful to have a plethora of subject matter experts (SMEs) across your business to get the biggest bang for your buck while building our your customer journey map -- this allows for maximum contribution in the shortest period of time. If you're a one man or woman band, then ask your partner or best friend to help you walk through it!

   d. Now that you have your buckets lined up and you are ready to roll, start thinking through every potential customer touchpoint that resides within your business today across all of those areas of your business and customer journey.

   e. Awareness bucket -- what are all of the different touchpoints that your company is doing today to create awareness? This is probably all of the different activities that your marketing efforts produce to try and capture potential customers attention. Examples include; sales assets, brochures, business cards, any type of marketing literature that you make available to leads interested in your business offerings.

f. **Consideration bucket** -- what are all of the different touchpoints that your customer might see or feel when trying to decide which company, solution or product they want to buy. Examples include; sales demo, cold calling, dropping by a customer office and showing them your product, information emails or mailers to encourage your customers towards their first purchase with your business

g. **Conversion bucket** -- what are all of the different customer touchpoints around actually converting a new customer? This might be revolve around the way that you think about your business funnel or pipeline to ignite new business. Every business has a slightly different pipeline strategy but the net of it is how do you pull a lead into an opportunity into an actual paying customer account? Examples include; Qualifying & disqualifying leads & opportunities, obtaining customer documents or payment information, getting your new customers setup and ready to buy within your business, etc.

h. **Onboarding bucket** -- what are all of the different customer touchpoints around onboarding and welcoming your new customers into your business? This concept tends to make or break most companies as they grow their customer portfolios. In short, companies that invest in the successful onboarding of their customers tend to focus on expectation setting, customer education and awareness, understanding their core needs and developing a true sustainable partnership into the future. I had a professor in college that always used this phrase with us "Proper, planning, prevents, poor performance". At the time I thought it was silly, as I proceeded through my own career and learned more about how the world and people inside of it actually works, he was spot on!

i. **Account Management bucket** -- once you bring a customer onboard and they are regularly using your product or service you need to start thinking about all of the customer touchpoints related to account management. This is essentially keeping all of the trains on the track and making sure that each buy is as smooth and seamless as the last. This is much easier said than done but in today's world we have access to so many incredible tools to make account management much easier. This might include CRM tools where you can house all of your customer information in one easy to use place, or an issue resolution management tool that allows you to keep track of every customer ticket whenever "something happens good or bad". Plus we have all kinds of amazing customer communications and scheduling tools that make it easier to make a stable of customers remain in the know and when key events are happening within your business. This tends to be one of the meaty areas of the customer journey map because most companies tend to house most of the day to day business doings inside of the account management camp. For example it's common to see account managers focused on buying, returns, billing, issue resolution, customer communications, product and technology refinement, customer surveying, etc.

j. **Customer loyalty bucket** -- this is one of the fun parts of every customer journey mapping exercise hearing all of the amazing ideas that people have around creating true customer loyalty. Once you've brought a customer through your funnel and into your customer portfolio, how do you keep them there for good? This is where customer loyalty comes into place -- for this section you need to consider all of the customer touchpoints that your business has for ensuring that customers remain loyal. It can be punch cards if you're a coffee shop (your 10th coffee on us) or if you're a software company maybe your customers get discounts for buying X # of seats. Airlines are famous for letting their customers rack up miles for future flight deals.

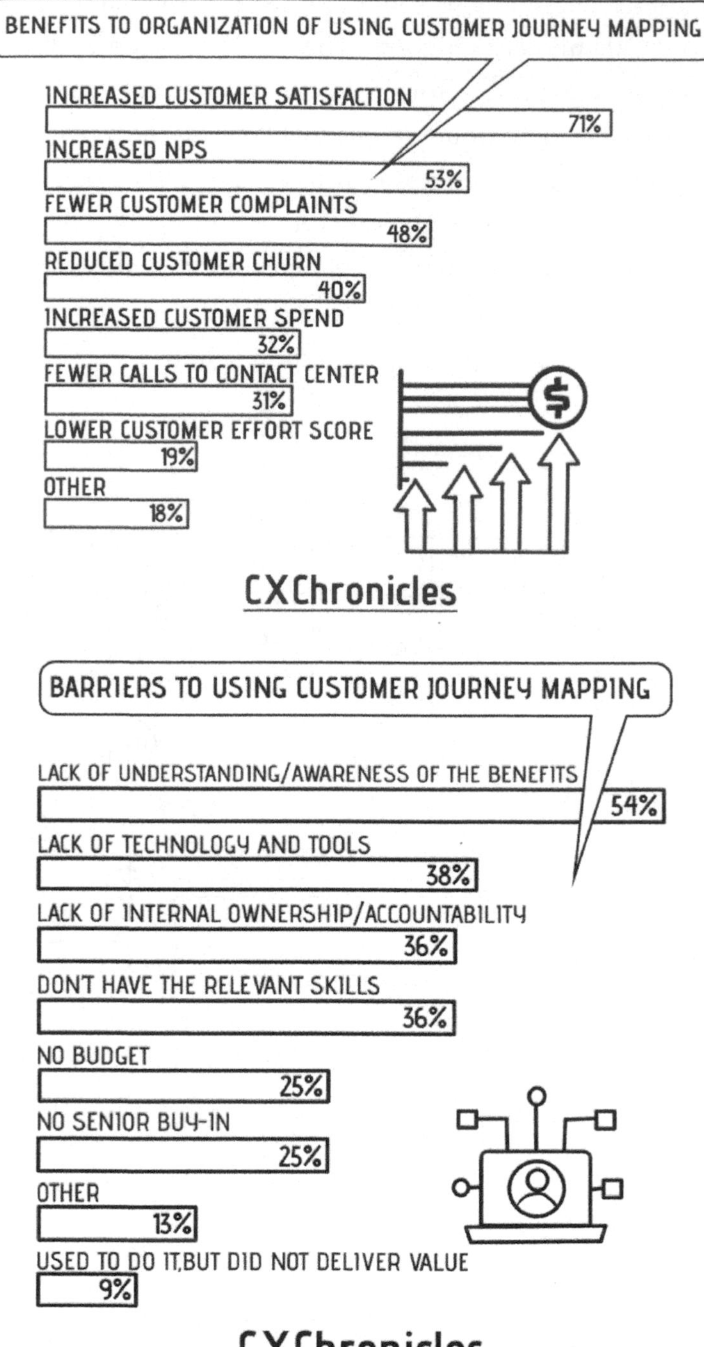
BENEFITS TO ORGANIZATION OF USING CUSTOMER JOURNEY MAPPING
INCREASED CUSTOMER SATISFACTION
71%
INCREASED NPS
53%
FEWER CUSTOMER COMPLAINTS
48%
REDUCED CUSTOMER CHURN
40%
INCREASED CUSTOMER SPEND
32%
FEWER CALLS TO CONTACT CENTER
31%
LOWER CUSTOMER EFFORT SCORE
19%
OTHER
18%
CXChronicles
BARRIERS TO USING CUSTOMER JOURNEY MAPPING
LACK OF UNDERSTANDING/AWARENESS OF THE BENEFITS
54%
LACK OF TECHNOLOGY AND TOOLS
38%
LACK OF INTERNAL OWNERSHIP/ACCOUNTABILITY
36%
DON'T HAVE THE RELEVANT SKILLS
36%
NO BUDGET
25%
NO SENIOR BUY-IN
25%
OTHER
13%
USED TO DO IT,BUT DID NOT DELIVER VALUE
9%
CXChronicles

After going through the CJM exercise for your business, you will have a true understanding of what your customers are experiencing while working with your company. There's always areas that jump off the wall as glaring opportunities for immediate change. Plus it highlights how complex and intricate these CJMs become as a company and customer base scale and grow into the future.

The deliverable of this CJM exercise should be a clean, clear, easy-to-digest map or document that walks the reader through the most recent version of the customer journey. It can be shared across leadership team and used on a regular basis to ensure that everyone within your company is on the same page about what an optimal customer journey needs to look like.

Plus companies are moving so quickly and are constantly evolving, that this exercise helps any leadership team to understand which areas of the business or customer experience are ripe for additional support, improvement or tools and technology to aid their cause!

Process Mapping

Where Design Thinking and Customer Journey Mapping focus on the customer, Process Mapping (sometimes referred to as flowcharts) focuses on the internal functions of your business. Once your company begins taking off, it's inevitable that your internal team will grow in conjunction. A growing team is a sign that your business is doing well and heading in the right direction, but it's also can be a huge challenge that involves employees and your customers!

Process maps can help any growing team in a variety of ways. First off, it defines how a team or department operates and what's expected of them along the way. If coupled with a flowchart, will also provide a visual for team reflection. Most importantly, will strive to improve efficiency.

Process mapping exercises can be conducted in any area of a business. Topics that are often ripe for process mapping include:

- Customer Pipeline
- Onboarding and Training
- Operations
- Billing and Payments
- Lead Generation

It's common for small companies to have 10 people working on the same team, but doing the tasks 10 different ways. This type of business behavior will not allow you to scale in an effectively: 10 different processes = 10 different results. Process mapping exercises allow businesses to create a level of consistency and a path for success. Process maps may include:

- Series of steps or points within a given process
- Often called flowcharts, providing a visual sense for a team or departmental process
- Identifies who or what is impacted by a given step
- Reveals areas of opportunity and advancement where performance or perception is low

I will leave you here with a process map for your next spaghetti or rigatoni (or "riggs") meal:

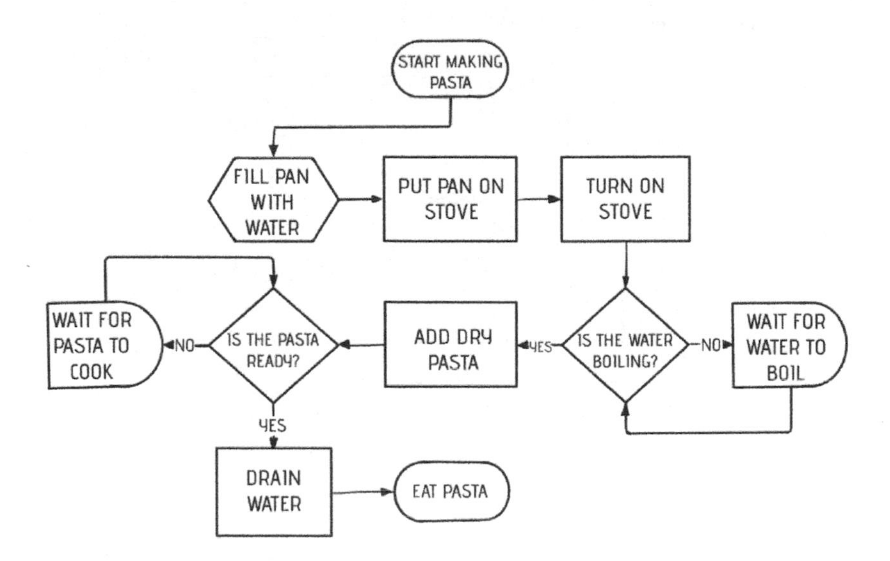

KPIs and Performance Metrics

KPIs and performance metrics that matter are a huge part of keeping track of your company's health. Just like a human body, a variety of vital signs help us understand how we are performing healthwise - the same is true in business performance. KPI is by definition a measurable value that helps a given business understand how it is performing in a given area. Each department or role - depending on its size and organizational complexity - should have its own KPIs that guide the overall direction and focus of the team.

Most sales organizations will focus on growth-based KPIs. These metrics can define whether or they are killing it or if they are about to be fired by the local carcass collector (i.e. sales manager). Here are some examples of growth-based KPIs:

- Number of sales activities
- Number of new marketing leads
- Number of new deals items sold
- Conversion rates
- Upselling and cross-selling opportunities

Operations teams, on the other hand, might think about fulfillment-based metrics:

- Number of items produced
- Number of new customers
- Number of touches

- Number of items delivered
- Issue resolution time
- Percentage of product satisfaction rates
- Percentage of error margin
- First contact rates

When thinking about your teams' KPIs, start off with company-wide performance metrics that the entire organization can have an impact on. Here are some examples:

1. Sales Volume ($)
2. Customer Retention (%)
3. Operational Efficiency (%)
4. Customer Satisfaction
5. Customer Engagement
6. Product or Service Performance

The common phrase what gets measured, gets managed is famous for one reason, it's true. Taking the time to understand which metrics & KPIs actually steer your business in the right direction is critical. Plus it allows you (even if on a simple level) to ensure that data, analytics and basic math drives your decision making each day as you grow your business.

Taking the time to measure the key metrics that drive your business, customer and employee experiences on a daily basis is critical for your success. I often used the analogy of sports for this focus area with past teams. Take a minute to think about your favorite sports team or athlete. Think about the way that they know every single possible stat that they measure for their given sport. These stats or performance metrics often fuel the difference for who the very best players are on the field vs. the worst. In football, for example the major KPIs might be the running back with the most TD's + yards rushed throughout the season. Or in soccer it's the player who has the most goals and assists. Without measuring these vital signs throughout the season we'd never really know the difference between the best and worst contributors, this same principle holds true for your business and team!

The Importance of Customer Onboarding

Customer onboarding has become a popular topic for conversation for most modern businesses, specifically software and service companies. With a plethora of technology at our fingertips, onboarding has become an artform. It includes properly setting expectations, ensuring the customer knows exactly how to interact with your company, and ensure that the relationship lasts well into the future.

Process: By far the most impressive customer onboarding experience that many of us know well, is with Apple products. From the box your iPhone is packaged to the order each item is removed from the box to the intuitive steps depicts on the phone screen. It makes setting up a new phone completely foolproof!

Many companies create a specific onboarding role to be the liaison that guides the customer through the step-by-step of getting started. Often times they work in conjunction with sales, account management, support and product. Companies that focus on their customer onboarding efforts see the following types of results early-on:

1. Reduced customer consternation
2. Reduced customer churn rates
3. Increased customer engagement
4. Increased quality for future account management placement (since you know the proper customer segment to best serve them)
5. Increased customer feedback about your company, product or service

Reflection: What do you do to ensure each new customer is positioned for success? Does your process make your customers feel appreciated out of the gates? Who do they interact within your business? Do you provide them any guides or materials?

Think of onboarding like your company's first impression or first date with a given customer. You need to knock it out of the park to get another shot with them! Remember, customers who don't have a great start with your company will not come back. Consider them gone for good!

If you have not done so already start mapping out your customer onboarding process from start to finish. What are all of the details within your customer's path to their first time buying experience? Do you have a flagging system or way to alert your team that this is a customer's first experience with your company? If you don't -- you need to get a basic plan in place ASAP to make sure that you are pulling out all of the stops signs when working with your company or startup!

Issue Resolution and Escalation Paths

Shaping the way your company thinks about issue resolution and customer escalations is critical as you begin to see significant growth or volume within any business. Think about the companies out there that you love to love - Zappos, Ritz Carlton, Apple, Uber, Facebook, Google - these companies are all excellent at issue resolution and escalation because they deal with day-to-day blocking and tackling required to deliver a great experience.

The way that a company handles its issue resolution and escalation paths tells you a lot about their leadership team and how they value and respect their given customer base, as well as their employees. Companies who take the time to build clearly defined and managed process maps for their high severity customer issues tend to blossom into sustainable businesses. Companies that don't usually end up in the trash bin!

Issue resolution is the way that your company manages customer issues, challenges, questions or concerns with your company's offerings. Having the ability to quickly understand that there's a customer issue, communicate with the customer about the fix and most importantly, keep the customer happy and ensure that they come back to your business in the future - it is the name of the game here, folks!

For many of you simply hearing the term "customer escalation" is enough to make you feel uncomfortable and look around the room as if something terrible just happened - and you should! Customer escalations are big, hairy, complex customer issues that arise within your business and require the involvement of upper management.

Depending on your specific customer base and organizational direction, customer escalations might happen in a variety of ways. The most common phrase that leads to a customer escalation is "Let me speak with your manager," but these are others I've heard throughout my tenure:

- "Get me your manager now, you stupid dickhead!"
- "Listen here you effin' jerk, give me your manager now!"
- "Will you put your manager on the phone before I go completely effin' crazy!!"
- And my personal favorite frustrated customer quote of all time: "Listen here, you fat blowjob fuck. I want to talk to your manager right now!"

Oddly enough, these interactions have always been my favorite part of working with customers. People are funny, unique animals when cornered or threatened in any way and they all react differently to different things, and it's important to remember that it's difficult to create a one-size fits all customer experience that suits everybody.

I love deescalating these types of situations and working with customers to bring them from a complete blinding rage right back down to planet earth in a cool, calm, collected fashion. You need to take the time to think through how your company will manage escalations. I look at customer escalations as the improve in customer experience.

When thinking about customer escalations, there's a level you can plan for and a level that is purely fly by the seat of your pants. Let's reuse the "5Ws & H" approach to outline how to think through customer escalations at your company:

1. **Who** do you want to escalate issues to?
2. **What** went wrong?
3. **Where** is the escalation being documented and logged? (CRM, email, phone calls, in-person meeting, etc.)
4. **Why** is this such a big problem?
5. **When** exactly did the issue occur?
6. **How** can we respond and improve things going forward?

Most companies approach the customer escalation process when the moment hits, but if you have at minimum an outline of the 5Ws & H, you'll be better positioned to continue that seamless customer experience we all strive to provide.

Reflection: Who manages these customer issues today? Is there a set process for what to do when these issues occur? How do you document and share when these instances occur? Are there KPI/performance metrics to keep track of them? Are there appropriate escalation paths in place to make sure our customers are always being heard?

Since this book is focused around helping you improve your company's overall customer experience and service efforts, here are key KPIs around issue resolution and escalation that you should focus on to improve your customer's overall experience with your business:

- **Call Abandonment Rates (%):** This is the percentage of inbound phone calls made to a call center that is abandoned by the customer before speaking to an agent. This is one of the most basic things you can do to be better than your competition. Answer the phones, folks!
- **Average Issue Resolution Time**: How long does it take your company to rebound from mistakes? Are you immediate or does it take a week to hear back from someone? Resolving issues in an expedient fashion is critical to gaining your customer's trust and respect!
- **Agent Response Time**: Let's say your customers leave you a voicemail or message via Facebook regarding your offerings - how fast do you actually get back to them with a response? This is a vital KPI to track because typically if you're not ready to chat when your customer is inquiring about something, oftentimes it's too late and they will go with one of your competitors who answered the phone on the first ring.
- **Customer Feedback (NPS/CSAT):** How do your customers think your company is doing? Do you take the time to ask your customers for feedback? This is super-important to make sure you understand exactly where your customers think you can improve!
- **Average # of agent touchpoints:** How many people on your team does it take to solve a problem or issue? Customers often prefer to speak with one agent or rep who can help them with their question from start to finish. Handoffs cause the potential for fumbles and fumbles or turnovers often leads to losing the game.

Take some time to think through basic KPIs that you can start building, measuring and sharing across your company. Remember your team and employees are always looking for feedback and ideas for how they can get better at their jobs. Share KPIs with them that will improve the overall product/service offering at your business. Better yet think about some ways that you might be able to incentivize your team for successfully executing these behaviors so they last well into the future!

Customer Pipeline Creation for Your Business

When building your business, it is important you define who you are building it for early-on. Successful businesses aren't just an idea that happened overnight, they consider a problem and an attractive solution to help their future customers. Every company should define an ICP: Ideal Customer Profile.

What's an ICP you ask? An ICP is the perfect type of customer or account for your specific business. An ideal customer profile checks all of the major boxes around how you or your business offerings can solve or ease specific problems. Imagine a laundry list of customer qualification checkboxes, the ICP literally is built for your business. The important thing to remember about ICPs is the more of them that you can load into your customer portfolios the easier it is to grow an army of brand ambassadors!

Defining this profile will allow your sales and customer service teams to focus on bringing as many of these folks into your customer portfolio, as possible. This doesn't mean you have to say no to customers that don't fit the ICP either - don't let me be misunderstood. But it is critical that you understand who the optimal customer is for your offering.

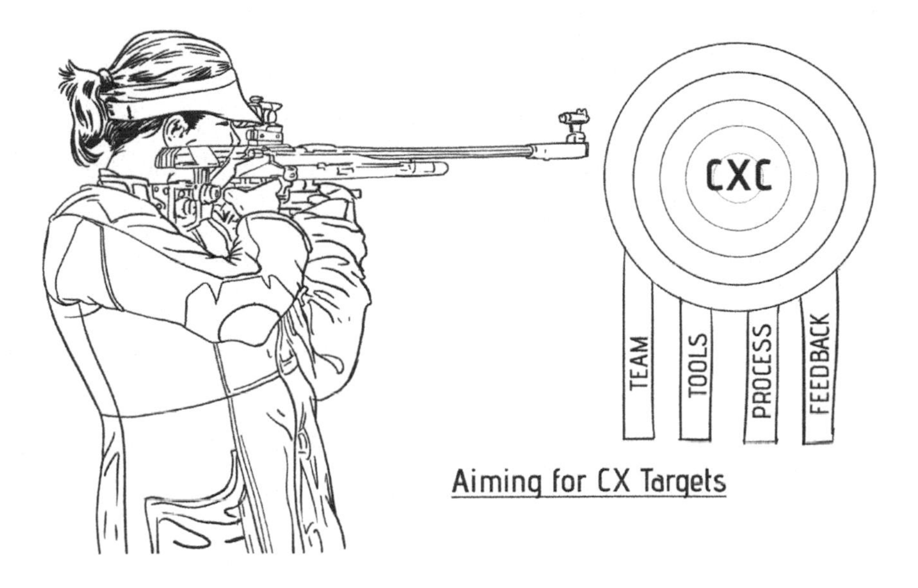

Aiming for CX Targets

Once you've defined your company's ICP, you can organize your pipeline. For example, many companies break a pipeline into the following components:

- Leads or Opportunities: These are potential customer targets that could lead to eventual new business.
- Customers or Accounts: These are active customers to your business.
- Customer Portfolios: A collection of specific customers or accounts that are similar in size, shape, expectations, and maybe even value (i.e. enterprise, mid-market)
- Former Customers or Churned Accounts: These are inactive, former customers who stopped using your business.

Depending on a company's size and industry focus, your customer pipeline might be laser-focused, but any company should be building and analyzing their customer pipelines.

The energy and effort that you put into building out your customer pipelines today will yield next month or even next quarter's wins. So remember that your business' pipeline creation is a critical piece to running your business and being able to make basic projections about where your future sales/revenue will be coming from!

Taking the time to map out and understand every aspect of your company's pipeline is another incredible opportunity for optimizing your business today and making sure that you fully understand the initial customer experience you've designed for your customers!

Reflection: Take some time with your team to run through every step of the onboarding and early sales experience with your business. How do they hear about you, where do they find you, how do they get in touch with you, etc?

CHAPTER SIX

Pillar Four - Feedback

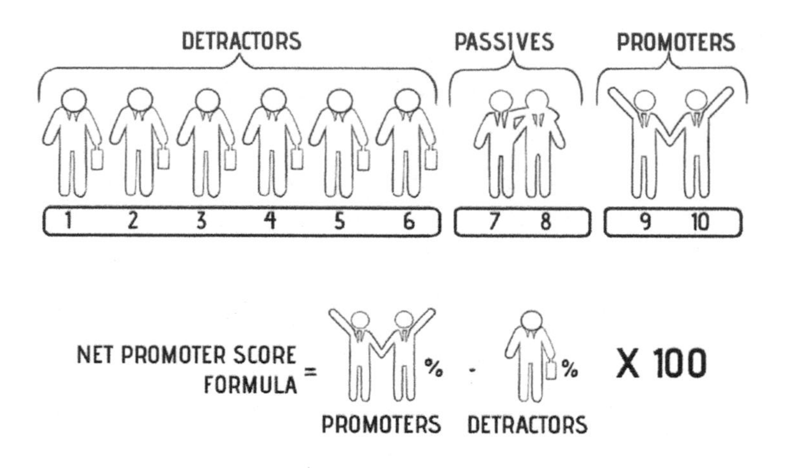

6

Pillar Four – Feedback

Feedback is one of the most important elements that we are going to discuss in this book - saved the best for last! When we talk about the feedback Pillar inside of the CX Nation, we have two different distinct datasets:

1. Employee Feedback: What are your employees saying?
2. Customer Feedback: What are your customers saying?

Employees who serve customers every day are your first line of defense and your most recognized ambassadors. Your employee's feedback is equally as valuable as your customers. Both are critical to any business that is serious about stepping up their CX game and bringing their company to the next level.

When it comes to customers, everything from who they are, where they are from, what makes them tick, and when they buy, is the ammo companies need to get folks to buy their offerings. As companies improve and master the art of data collection, they continuously improve their ability to know the customer inside and out. There's been a ton of value placed around understanding your customers - this is why customer data is often referred to as "modern day oil!"

Feedback from your customers and employees gives your business an accurate depiction of reality related to your company's offerings. These groups know your business better than anyone because they're living with it each and every day. Often times, business leaders look at the top line and assume the company is killing it and on its way to becoming the 800-lb gorilla in your space, but watch out! Do your customers and employees actually agree with you?

Reflection: When was the last time that you sent out a customer survey? Do you regularly get pulse checks from your employees? What type of questions are you asking? What do you do with that information after its collected?

Employee Feedback

Many leaders of the world's largest companies harp on how critical it is to invest in your staff. Some companies do an incredible job with this. For example, Google host weekly speakers, classes and continuous improvement activities to ensure that their staff is properly trained on the continuous personal development path.

On the other hand, most small businesses and startups have a reputation of being so focused on growth, raising the next investment round or winning the next big client that they spend little to no time investing in their staff and ensuring that they are given access to different mediums that will allow them to grow and build out their personal playbooks.

The funny thing is investing in your staff, listening to their thoughts and ideas, and pushing them to take ownership of your customers and accounts is one of the simplest ways of developing a strong foundation for your customer experience. Employees who are properly vetted, trained, supported and managed will care more about their jobs, your company and, most importantly, your customers!

With that being said, employee feedback is critical to collect as your company scales and here are ways I've found successful:

- Weekly 1:1s: This is critical to ensure that there is a cadence for managers to spend time with each teammate to listen, learn and understand what's happening inside of their day-to-day (good, bad and ugly). There's no excuse not to do this!

- Weekly Team Meetings: Each department or group would gather regularly and discuss success stories, challenges, roadblocks, and brainstorm opportunities for improvement. There are often golden ideas that come from these meetings!
- All-Hands or All-Company Meetings: From time to time - minimally monthly - company leaders should be rally the entire staff and share the overall direction and performance of the business. This keeps the lines of communication open between leadership and the front lines ensuring that people have the platform to speak up and ask questions.
- Employee Feedback Surveys: These are becoming increasingly popular for employers to learn more about how their staff is doing and how they think the overall direction of the company is going. Some companies will convert this into employee NPS surveys or even simple polls to aggregate what the team is thinking and saying about your business. Pay attention to this feedback - your staff knows your customers and business processes better than anyone!

Employee Net Promoter Score (ENPS)

Employee net promoter scores (ENPS) have become increasingly popular especially with technology and software companies. Most business leaders understand that having a clear view of what your employees think about the way things are working for your customers is one of the most valuable insights.

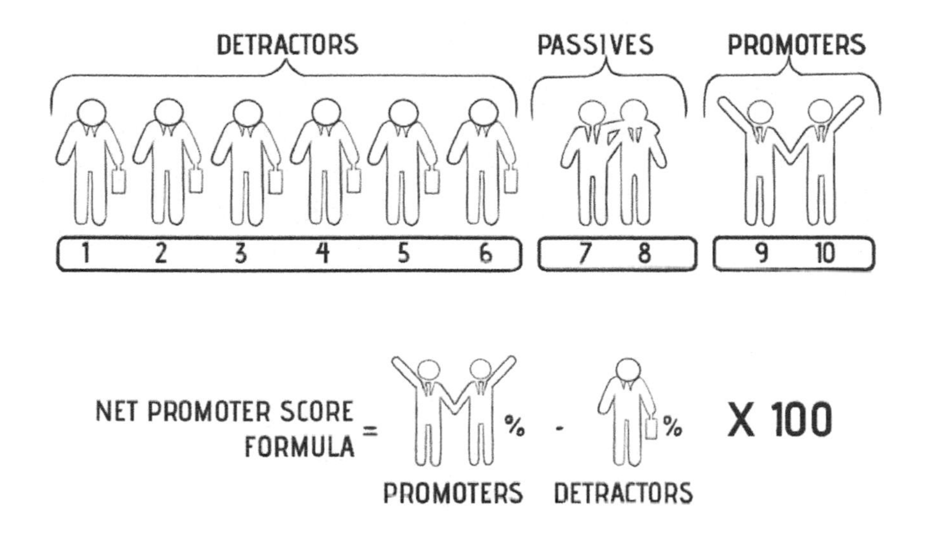

To start, employees spend the bulk of their time doing nothing but interacting with your customers. They know the good, the bad, and the ugly about your business - there's no hiding the dirty underwear with this group, folks!

The employees who are involved, informed, and included in your overall customer experience design will remain invested in helping you build your business. And those who are not taken care of, listened to, acknowledged and most importantly, properly compensated, will never grow deep roots within your business. They will also have a tendency towards treating your customers in a highly transactional type of way.

If your company hasn't done so already, take time to send a basic survey on how things are going within your business. Make sure that you let your team know that you want honest, constructive feedback and that you're going to listen to what they say to improve your business!

Lastly, you must remember that involvement - as it relates to teamwork and building - is one of the easiest ways of keeping folks who work inside of your business engaged, interested and ready to come to crush it at each and every work day! In the next section, we will cover how net promoter scores are calculated!

Customer Feedback

Remember both internal and external feedback drives process optimization! When it comes to types of customer feedback reporting types, there is a wide variety. In this section, we will go into detail about some of the most popular feedback methods.

WHAT HAPPENS AFTER
POOR CUSTOMER EXPERIENCE

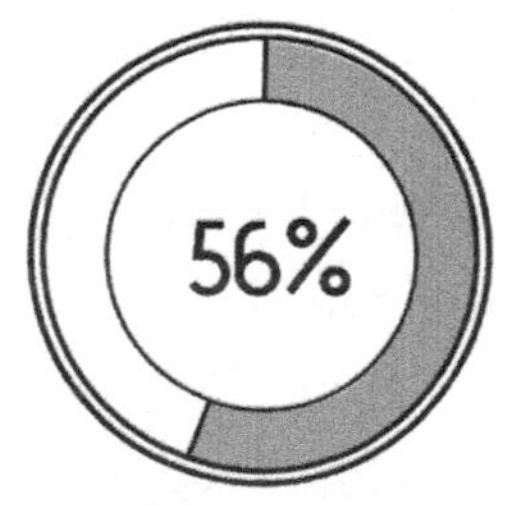

WILL NEVER USE THE COMPANY AGAIN

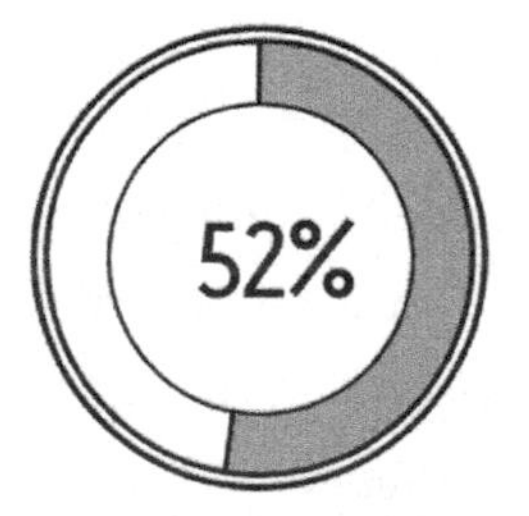

WILL TELL FAMILY & FRIENDS ABOUT THE EXPERIENCE

54%

WILL ESCALATE TO A SUPERVISOR OR MANAGER

Net Promoter Score (NPS)

To start, one of the most popular customer feedback reporting types that customer experience leaders use is the Net Promoter Score (NPS). NPS is one of the simplest ways for you to begin establishing your customer feedback reporting for your business. The NPS score - similar to CSAT reporting (customer satisfaction) - provides a numeric approach to understanding how your customers really feel about your company. NPS is calculated based on responses to a single question: *How likely is it that you would recommend our company to a friend or colleague?* The scoring for this answer is most often based on a 0 to 10 scale. Most often, these questions are sent right after the provided offering is received - whether by email, text, or phone.

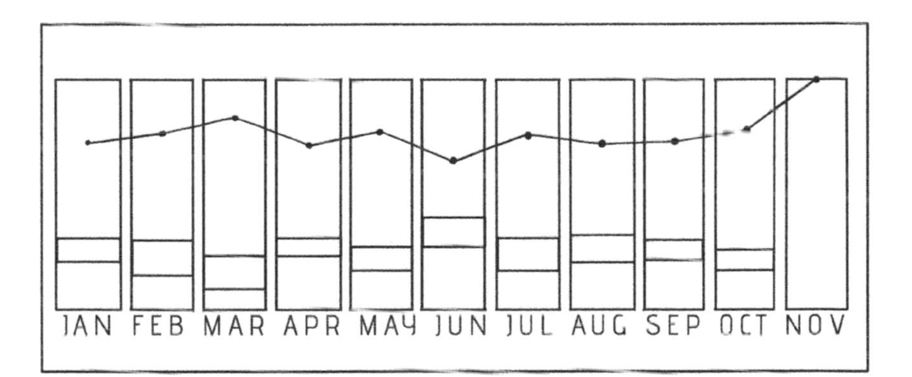

Measuring Your Monthly NPS Scores

Establishing an NPS score for your business immediately separates you from the rest of the pack because you have a quantified, data-fueled reporting baseline for how your company fairs today. Better yet, you can actually break these NPS survey reports into specific focused areas that allow you to see how your customers feel about different parts of your organization throughout the customer journey.

When it comes to calculating the feedback, there are three types of responses: promoters, passives, and detractors.

- Promoters: Those who respond with a score of 9 to 10 - "Boom, you're killing it!"
- Passives: Those who respond with a score of 7 and 8 - "OK, we'll keep trying to wine and dine you."
- Detractors: Those who respond with a score of 0 to 6 - "Ouch, you don't like us, but why?"

So how does the calculating work? Let's say that your company sets up an NPS survey and gets the following response breakdowns:

- (80) promoters or 80%
- (10) passives or 10%
- (10) detractors or 10%
- (100) total responses or 100%

Your company's NPS for that given time period is going to be 70 NPS.

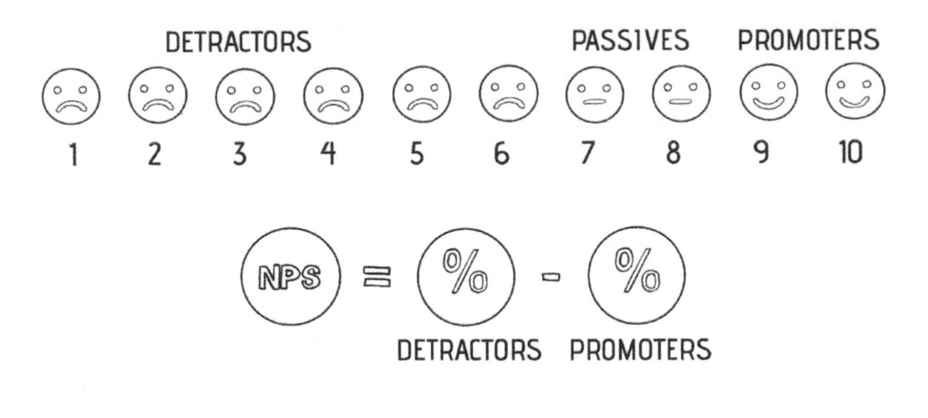

<u>Promoters - Detractors</u>

<u>**Customer Satisfaction (CSAT)**</u>

Customer Satisfaction (CSAT) reporting is a term often used in marketing when a company is thinking about whether their given product or service is meeting or, better yet exceeding customer's expectations. This reporting measures the short-term happiness, or how a customer feels about a specific service or product - unlike NPS, it does not address how a customer feels about a company as a whole. So keep in mind, the question asked will vary based on the services or product consumed. CSAT is calculated by the number or percentage of customers whose reported customer experience exceeds specific satisfaction goals.

For example, Property Armor Management takes care of rental properties in New York and Florida cleaning homes, managing keys, mowing the lawn, cleaning the pool, etc.. Some CSAT questions for Property Armor might include:

- Does Property Armor clean and prepare our home for guests and meet our standard of cleaning expectations?
- Does Property Armor clean my pool thoroughly?
- Does Property Armor keeps our property booked, guests happy and rental income coming on time?

Typically use a 1-5 rating system with 1 being very dissatisfied and 5 being very satisfied. Respondents are asked to rate their experience using this scale, although scales can vary by company. The scores are then averaged and converted into a percentage with 0% being complete dissatisfaction and 100% being complete satisfaction.

CSAT image (Customer Satisfaction)

Customer Effort Score (CES)

Customer Effort Score (CES) is another effective type of customer satisfaction survey that measures the ease or difficulty of using a given product or service based on a scale of "very easy" to "very difficult."

Some studies suggest CES scores are better predictors of customer loyalty and retention trends versus CSAT or NPS feedback. The rationale being CES scores capture direct feedback around a specific engagement. By simplifying the customer journey and reducing friction within each customer touchpoint, you increase the chances of producing positive customer interactions with a given product or service. Typically, CES are captured right after a customer interacts with a product or connects with your CX team.

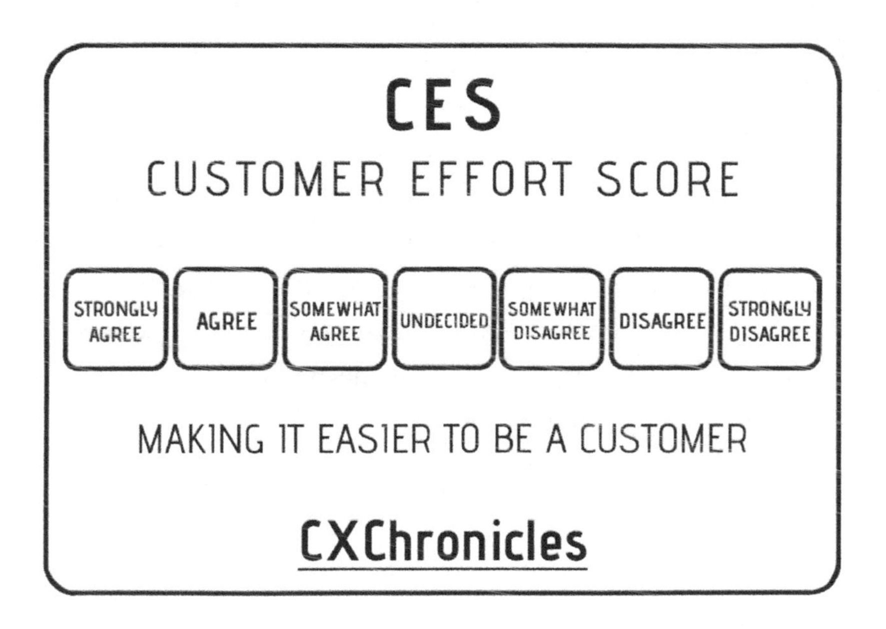

Feedback on Social Media

Mediums like Facebook, Twitter, Instagram and others have changed the game for how customers can quickly provide real-time feedback for how a given company is performing. Whether customers are "checking-in" on Facebook or sharing pictures of their mountain of mozzarella sticks on Instagram, we are living in a time where everything is real-time and expectations are high for immediate satisfaction. With a blink of an eye, one bad customer experience can be shared with thousands - better yet, millions - and can dramatically impact the success of your business.

If you haven't taken time to manage your social media strategy, you should do so immediately! Having a strong social presence helps solidify your business' credibility. As future potential customers contemplate buying from you, they will undoubtedly check out your FB page, Instagram page or Twitter feed.

Responding to negative reviews is simply part of the modern business world and it's common for companies to have a firm policy on how they manage the responses to negative social media posts. And it is vital that you respond to it as quickly as possible. Never fight back or trade blows with your customers, but acknowledge the issue and try to get that customer on the phone to remediate the issue or challenge faced. Other customers and potential customers will see how your business responded and feel comfortable with the fact that the organization put its best foot forward to solve the issues - that gains your business credibility alone.

Don't let your customers walk out the door!

Customer Churn

Customer Churn (a.k.a. customer attrition) is the loss of a client or customer and it can be due to a variety of reasons. Churn is any business' worst nightmare - you want to focus in on this metric right out of the gates and never lose sight of it! We all know that it is cheaper and easier to keep a current customer happy than to go and acquire a new one to bring into your customer portfolio.

churn = you losing customers

In short, churn can be measured by how many total customers you have at the start of the month versus the end of the month. For example, let's say that Hinton's Laundry has 100 customers on January 1st and by February 1st there's 105 recurring customers. This would be great news because this means that Hinton's customer base actually grew over the course of the month!

Now here's another example.

Let's say that Hinton's has 100 customers on January 1st and by February 1st, there's only 90 customers. This would be horrible news because it would mean that Hinton's customer base shrank by nearly 10%! Now if you have 10% less customers then you did last month, what do you think happens to your company's bottom line? Or what happens to your take-home check as the business owner when your churn rate is getting out of control?

Reflection: Do you know your company's churn rate? Do you know how many customers you had last quarter vs. now? Do you know the amount of revenue over given months? How are you tracking churn? What initiatives are in place to improve those numbers?

In the world of churn, there are two main types that you should be aware of: Active and Passive Churn.

Active Churn or Controllable Churn is when customers leave your company for reasons that are in your control - i.e. billing errors, late delivery, communication breakdown, multiple instances of dissatisfaction.

Passive Churn or Uncontrollable Churn is when client matters that you simply cannot control - i.e. client goes out of business, client passes away, client was never truly qualified or segmented for success.

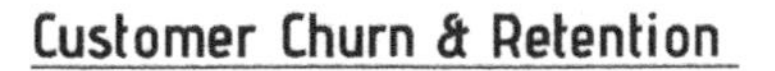

Customer Churn & Retention

So how do you get your company's arms around customer churn? We touched on KPIs earlier but here are commonly monitored KPIs related to customer churn and retention:

- Portfolio Size: The number of customers inside an agents' book of business
- Onboarding Rate: The number of customers each agent brings on each month
- LTV: The Lifetime Value of a customer in revenue
- Upselling/Cross-Selling: New deals or revenue that your team is able to sell to your existing customers (i.e. additional services, add-on products, etc.)
- Issue Resolution/Ticket Management: How quickly can your team resolve customer issues?
- NPS/CSAT/Customer Feedback reporting: The type of feedback your customers consistently provide

Below are specific CX KPIs related to customer churn and retention:

- Average Ticket Count: How many issue tickets can an agent manage a day?
- Daily Ticket Totals: How does this daily ticket or case load vary?
- First Contact Rate: How quickly does it take a customer to connect with your business?
- Average Issue Resolution Time: How fast can your team resolve customer issues?
- Number of Touchpoints per Inquiry: On average, how many connects does it take to solve one customer issue?

- Ticket Close Rate: How quickly can your team resolve a ticket from open to close?
- Ticket Segmentation: Where does your company see the bulk of its issues?
- Ticket Resolution by Segment: What ways does your company solves customer issues by team?
- Ticket Resolution by Agent: How does each agent perform here?

LTV, CAC, MRR and Other Wild Acronyms

Below are some customer-focused critical concepts and acronyms that many business leaders have to think about on a regular basis to ensure their overall performance is heading in the right direction. Take some time to think through the terms below and how they might relate to your business. Are you already tracking some of these items?

- LTV: Lifetime Value of a Customer
- CAC: Customer Acquisition Costs
- MRR: Monthly Recurring Revenue
- NPS: Net Promoter Score
- CSAT: Customer Satisfaction
- CES: Customer Effort Scores

Get to know these different measures because they make a huge impact on investor decisions, executive recruitment, and the general success path of any business you join now or in the future.

One of the easiest ways that you can get better at thinking about how to use customer feedback is reflecting on past customer interactions to gain insights and next steps for optimization or re-design. Ideally, your company has access to customer data - even if it's a simple spreadsheet. It is important to get into the habit of regularly diving into feedback to establish trends - good, bad and ugly - for what your customers think about your business.

As you master your feedback collection skills, identify who within the organization needs to be aware of such findings. How do you bring it up and down the organizational chart in any business? Who needs to know what, who should be involved, who are the chief stakeholders? These individuals are going to be the drivers of change within your organization.

The next level of this practice is to create a culture laser-focused on "full-circle feedback". From the customer to your staff and leadership team, always think about easy ways to inject the easy wins back into future product/service offerings.

Stay fresh in how your company obtains this customer feedback - maybe use online surveys, mailers, personal calls or even focus groups. Feedback is important. Listening to customers is so key, but remember that it's up to you and your leadership to remain focused on what you actually do with that customer feedback. Leaving it in a Google Doc and doing nothing with it will not provide much positive gains.

CHAPTER SEVEN

Quickly Put The Four CX Pillars™ to Work

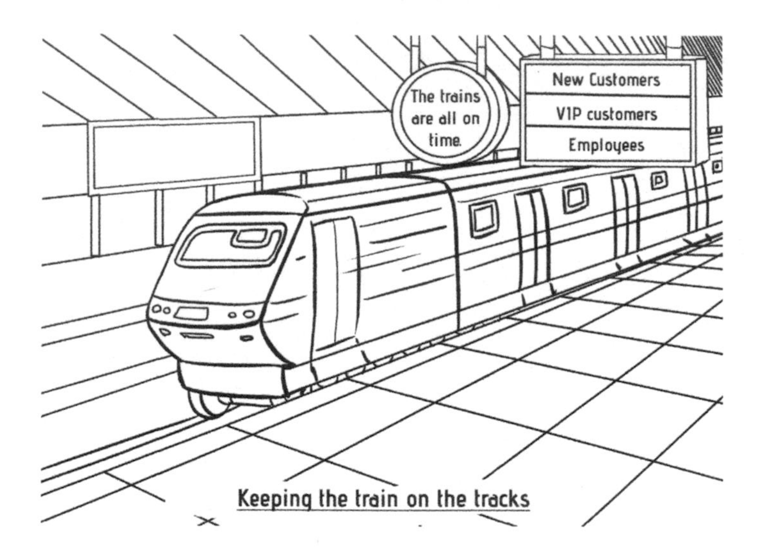

7

Quickly Put The Four CX Pillars™ to Work

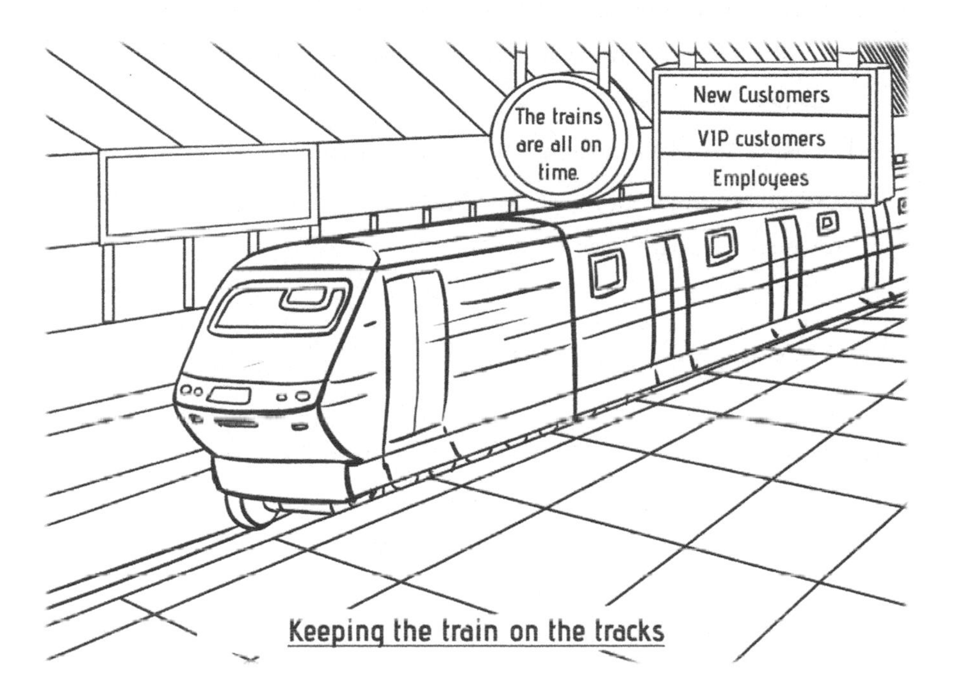

Now that you are a master of The Four CX Pillars™ and understand where to point all of your focus, time and energy to manage your business moving forward, let's get into the nuts and bolts of how we put The Pillars to work. Keep in mind, depending on the size of your company and your team, each one of you will have a different path for how The Four CX Pillars™ guide your business to the promised land. Here are some ways to start thinking about The Four CX Pillars™ within your organization:

Pillar One - Team:

1. Dedicate time every week to connect with your team, whether individually or as a group.
2. Invest in continuously learning and improvement for your team members - prove there is opportunity to grow within your business.
3. Always seek to recruit and find new talent.
4. Study how your competition finds talent and build upon that process to create your own.

Pillar Two - Tools:

1. Keep all your customer information in one easy-to-access place.
2. Know the status of your new opportunities, orders, and existing customers at all times.
3. Dedicate time each month exploring new tools and technology that might help to grow your business.

Pillar Three - Process:

1. Create and document your Standard Operating Procedures (SOPs) to have a clear expectations for you, your staff, and, most importantly, your customers!

2. Build your first customer journey map - if you have already, do it again!
3. Always be improving! Continuous improvement is mandatory to growing your business and sharpening the pencil with how your company operates.

Pillar Four - Feedback:

1. Conduct internal and external surveys (customer and employee).
2. Create a regular cadence for feedback review and initiatives. Appoint a team to help drive change from these reviews.
3. Share feedback internally and externally. Customers like companies that show they care!

Like anything else in business, sports or life -- you have to start somewhere! Taking the first steps are often the most difficult but once you find your cadence it becomes easier to walk, jog and eventually run towards your objectives and goals.

Working and using the Four CX Pillars methodology into your business is the exact same type of thing. Use the above steps and make them your own style, flavour and preferences. Take some time to vet these pillars with your team and see what they think. Try to listen for their ideas around how this might simplify their day to day efforts and allow them to compartmentalize all of the daily stressors that impact them.

And for God's sake at least try to utilize and incorporate some of these learnings and findings into your business!

CHAPTER EIGHT

CX Lessons & Advice from The CX Nation

8

CX Lessons & Advice from The CX Nation

In this chapter, I wanted to give a shout out to the amazing founding members of the "CX Nation." These are customer minded business leaders across the world who have dedicated their careers to improving the way customers interact and communicate with companies.

Since launching CXChronicles in 2018, we've talked with business leaders from companies like Zappos, Betterment, Comcast, G2Crowd, Vimeo, Thumbtack, Ebay, Microsoft, Grindr, Greenhouse, and a plethora of amazing startups all around the world!

We've also hosted a number of best-selling authors and experts on the customer experience and service space including Shep Hyken, John DiJulius, Jeff Gothelf, Dan Gingiss and Roger Dooley.

We thought it would be a pretty cool section to provide you with some mini-CX lessons and tips straight from the mouths of the CX Nation.

Lesson 1: CX Worst Practices

Here's what you shouldn't do with your customers. Review these with youR customer-facing teams and make sure that you are not committing any of these common fouls!

1. Lie: This is one of the worst things you can do! Customers always appreciate honesty.
2. Difficult to contact: Don't make this a game of hide and seek.
3. Be defensive: Getting upset, talking back with a customer, telling them they are wrong. This will kill any business!
4. Not update your customers: Don't keep your customers hanging!
5. Settle for the bare minimum: You need to go above and beyond for your customers, this day and age. Strive to wow!

6. Rely on chatbots: Fully automating your support takes time, plus you will always have customers that want a real person to connect with.
7. Not trust your CX team: Let your team make some of these tough customer decisions.
8. Not treat customers like real people: Customers appreciate empathy!
9. Not focus on customer retention: Keeping existing customers is always cheaper than acquiring new ones.

Lesson 2: 10 Signs Your Business Should Invest in CX Technology

If your business is beginning to feel any of the following friction points, you might want to start thinking about finding the right customer relationship manager solution to help grow your business.

1. Everyone in your business works with customers in inconsistent ways.
   a. Put best practices in place for how your staff works and speaks to your customers.
2. There's uncertainty of how engaged your customers are.
   a. You need to know if your customers are using your product/service. What do they like/dislike?
3. Your team doesn't have access to real-time customer information.
   a. You need the basic components of what's going on with each customer to best serve them.
   b. Understand the Who-What-Where-When-How (Introduction).

4. Your team is burdened with mundane, administrative, time-consuming tasks.
    a. Difficult to manage customer communications volume
    b. Difficult to focus on customer service and quality with rising volume
5. Team members can't easily segment or place customers in pre-designed buckets.
    a. Customer segmentation is a critical process that allows you to understand who's who inside of your customer portfolio. For example; high value customers might get priority, where lower-value accounts might have a different set of service options and service level agreement (SLA)
6. Your team is reactive and late to respond to customer issues.
    a. Customers are not able to easily get in touch with your business
    b. Multiple touchpoints (phone calls, emails, texts, or in-person customer communications, etc.)
7. Your sales or success team is struggling to upsell or retain your best customers.
8. Indicators for customer success are difficult to define, measure or track.
    a. Struggling to establish KPIs
    b. No clear customer data
9. Your Team is Missing Important Customer Milestones.
    a. Critical customer celebration points.
    b. Onboarding, anniversary, number of purchases, birthdays, press releases.
    c. Celebrate the milestones -- phone calls, emails, etc.
10. Customer feedback is beginning to sour!

a. Once you detect that your customer feedback is beginning to sour, it is imperative to start making adjustments

b. Identify the top themes or focus areas that seem to be creating the most friction

c. Start making subtle changes to improve the overall situation -- always let your customers know that you are listening and working off of their valued feedback!

Lesson 3: Four CX Myths that are Holding Your Business Back!

1. Angry Customers are a lost cause!
   a. Not true. These are the customers you should learn from. Oftentimes these folks will provide feedback.
   b. Huge win: Getting a customer to come back from the dead!
2. Sticking to one formula is the way to go.
   a. The reality is you need to be flexible with a customer.
   b. Process and workflow guides everything for your team and customers.
   c. Curve balls will continue to get whipped at your heads every day.
   d. Always be improving!
3. Marketing is more important than customer experience.
   a. Sales, Marketing, and CX are all under one roof on the revenue team. We're in it together!
4. Customer Complaints are Bad for Business.
   a. No one likes to see customer complaints. Take it as feedback. Learn from it and embrace it.

My hope is that these lessons ignite additional parting ideas around how you should be thinking about the build out and design of your company's CX and customer-centric approach moving forward. Here are some more quick tips from The CX Nation:

- Your customer is everything. They are the lifeblood of the business!
- The leadership team has the responsibility to keep the focus on being customer-centered!
- Loyalty is key - focus on building customer loyalty.
- Be relentless with figuring out how to make your customers happy - even when it seems impossible.
- Leaders that know what's going on with their customers are the most successful.
- Bringing a churned customer back is one of the biggest wins in CX - aim for win-backs, baby!
- Be flexible with your customers. Curve balls will get whipped at you - be creative and maintain the customer's trust!
- Great CX is the combo of design thinking and sound marketing efforts.
- Customers want to feel heard. Let them speak and listen. Empathy goes a long way!
- Don't be affected by "no" - rejection builds confidence!
- Provide a great customer experience before they're a customer.

CHAPTER NINE

The Continuous Improvement Never Stops!

9

The Continuous Improvement Never Stops!

Now that you have an understanding of The Four CX Pillars™ and begin to implement best practices in place, it is vital to perform on-going assessments in your ongoing CX performance.

Vince Lombardi used to say that "Perfection is not attainable, but if we chase perfection we might catch excellence." It doesn't matter what your business or industry is, customers can tell instantly if your business or company is chasing perfection or simply going through the motions. If you want your company or business to succeed and last for the long-haul start aiming for perfection!

The ongoing assessment is critical to ensure that you have a basic control and monitoring plan for all of the items that you tackle within The Four CX Pillars™. By continuously evaluating The Four CX Pillars™, you are forcing your organization to remain focused on your delivery with customers. Companies that are constantly optimizing and iterating get ahead of their competition and remain better positioned to win!

Continuous improvement is an organizational way of remaining fit and ready for any market changes, customer preference shifts, employee relation changes and basically anything that might (and will) get thrown towards your company or team's future progress.

We often refer to our client CI (continuous improvement) initiatives as "spring or fall training opportunities" similar to that of baseball or football. Another way of thinking about the importance of injecting CI initiatives into your company's growth plans are to imagine yourself (or your team) as a boxer or MMA fighter preparing for the next big fight. The fighter goes through an incredible period in which they chanel all of their focus and energy into evolving into their own version of championship form. It might happen through early morning runs, weight lifting sessions late into the night or hitting the heavy back until your knuckles are literally bruised and battered. All of these activities are making you better, faster, stronger. CI is your tool for getting into fighting shape as an organization and ready for your next big fight or challenge.

Championship form comes different to every person and every business -- for some of you reading this book, you are simply trying to figure out ways of winning (or keeping) your first couple of customers. For others you are trying to think about ways that you can manage the thousands (or maybe even millions) of customers that you've circled the wagons on today!

Here are some basic Continuous Improvement ideas for you to build within your business or team:

Take 5 minutes to visualize how each one of these exercises might work within your business.

1. VOC Exercises -- "Voice of Customer"
   a. Take time to regularly listen to what your customers are saying
   b. Design a team or special unit dedicated to understanding customer feedback and sentiment
   c. Take time building regular surveys or calling campaigns to better understand your customer and their needs
   d. Create dashboards and visibility points across your business!
2. VOE Exercises -- "Voice of Employee"
   a. Take time to regularly listen to what your employees are saying
   b. Design a team or special unit dedicated to understanding employee feedback and sentiment.
   c. Your team often understands customers better than anyone as they work hand in hand with them every day
   d. Create regular feedback loops for employees to make sure they feel heard!
3. State of Unions Across Teams or Departments
   a. Impose or create regular team and department huddles
   b. Install that communication across teams and departments is of paramount success
   c. Build a culture that prides itself on optimal communication
   d. Kill it with your all-hands game!
4. OKR and Strategic Visions -- Objectives and Key Results
   a. Create simple,understandable objectives and key results for your team to follow

b. Pick no more than 5 major goals for your team to focus on for a given period of time (quarters or for the business year)

c. Make sure that everyone in the company is fully aware of what this entails and how they will specifically contribute to achieving these goals!

There a number of other ways that you can utilize the CI strategies that have worked for so many successful entrepreneurs before us. Be creative along the way with your team and always figure out how you can make time to sharpen your axes.

If you found The Four CX Pillars™ model helpful and want to expand your CX optimization efforts, CXChronicles offers additional resources to our clients. Some of our offerings include:

- CX Scorecards: CXChronicles' CX assessment tool to evaluate the health of your CX and customer service operations.
- EX Scorecards: CXChronicles' EX assessment tool to evaluate the health of your EX employee experience and operations
- CX Implementation Plans: CXChronicles' consultative services to work alongside your team to develop a full CX strategy.
- CX Roadmaps: CXChronicles's consultative services which collaborates with your leadership team to optimize key pain points as it relates to CX and customer service.
- CXChronicles Video Training Series: Custom CX training videos for your company
- CXChronicles Team Training and Consulting Projects can include:
  - The Four CX Pillars™ Presentation
  - Customer Journey Mapping Exercise

  - ○ Process Mapping Exercise
  - ○ Voice of Customer Exercise
  - ○ Customer Team Playbook Creation and Implementation
  - ○ Customer Churn Reporting
  - ○ NPS & CSAT Scoring and Reporting
- The CXChronicles Podcast: Weekly podcast with customer-minded business leaders
  - ○ Discuss The Four CX Pillars™
  - ○ Share CX Weekly Updates: highlighting news in the CX world

As we conclude the "Four CX Pillars To Grow Your Business" ™ it's important to make sure that we set in stone some of the major themes and ideas for you to take away from this book.

#1 -- Team is everything!

All of you have heard a million times throughout your personal journeys that nothing is more important than family and friends. In the world of business your team is your family and friends. They will pick you up while you're down and they will pull you back down to earth when you're head is getting so big that it's pulling you off the ground. Your team is the front line chain to your overall business success -- if there are weak links in the chain there will in fact be breaks along the way. Do your absolute best as a Four CX Pillar leader to maintain the strongest "human chain" as possible at all times!

#2 -- Tools will make you or break you!

Most successful companies that get ahead do so by building best in class tool-kits for their customers and employees to manage their day to day business operations. It might be the way that you build out and organize your CRM system or the way that you manage all of your inbound customer communications. Industry leading tool-kits tend to get industry leading results. Set your sights high when building out your company's tool kit for the future.

#3 -- Process and workflows for creating dominating customer experiences

Taking the time to build and optimize living playbooks, standard operating procedures and the rules of engagement for how your customers will best come to experience your business are key to success. Taking the time to get all of the best practices and tribal knowledge in one easy to use, easy to access place is one of the easiest ways for creating consistent, remarkable customer and employee experiences.

#4 -- Feedback is fuel for your company's future growth

At CXChronicles we are constantly talking about how customer and employee feedback is like modern day fuel for growing and scaling your business and team. It's never been easier than it is today to collect, manage and understand mountains of data about your customers and employees and their regular behaviors that drive your business. It is imperative that you take time while building your company to review what this feedback suggests and indicates, learn how you and your team can improve from it, learn how to ignore the unhelpful trollish feedback that today's internet brings and constantly be pushing ahead with understanding how feedback is littered with nuggets or golden opportunity for you to build off of with your team!

I'd like to wrap up this book with a short story to illustrate how the simple decision to either focus on your customers and employees from day one can have a strong impact on your business.

> *There are two business owners who both knew that eventually they would need to think about how they could get their arms around building out their CX strategy for the future.*
>
> *The first business owner, Tony, was adamant that the only way that he would be able to protect and maintain everything that he had built was by establishing a dedicated team to provide their customers with a memorable experience.*

It didn't even matter if Tony was focused on sales or operations. In fact, he was focused on both to ensure that his company was in a position where, regardless of whatever customer request or task was, they could quickly and swiftly manage it to resolution with ease.

For this CX unit it didn't matter whose job it was or which department should be the ones to "own or manage it," Rather, they developed a simple attitude of "let's get this job done -- hoorah!!!!"

And that attitude became contagious throughout Tony's business and team. It didn't matter what challenges they faced. They swung the sword through the zombie's head and got the job done, and guess who felt it more than anyone? The customers who supported and frequented Tony's company again and again.

The second business owner's name was Ralphie. He started his business for one reason: make those dollar dollar bills squeal baby regardless of the cost! He wanted to make it rain all over the place and guess who he didn't give a care about? His customers or his people -- the folks that would manage these customers day in and day out. Ralphie was more focused on making his luxury car payments and calling Blade Helicopters to come pick him and his friends up from some rooftop by helicopter in some concrete jungle.

Needless to say Ralphie didn't take the time like Tony to develop a robust, detailed plan and strategy for ensuring that his customers and his people were taken care of, constantly managed, and hand-held each and every day. Specifically, Ralphie didn't take the time to develop and build-out the Team, Tools, Process and Feedback measures required to ensure that his business would last well into the future!

Who would you want to get your end-of-day work drinks with? Tony or Ralphie?

For those thinking about building their own startup company or their own team inside of an existing company, take what you've learned and apply it into something useful and practical that applies to your individual craft or trade. Don't be afraid to start testing these ideas inside of your business. You don't have to flip the CEO's desk over and smash in the computer screen to get these points across either, although that would be pretty comical!

Keep things simple folks. You have The Four CX Pillars™ to focus on:

1. TEAM
2. TOOLS
3. PROCESS
4. FEEDBACK

Even if all you do is develop a simple one-page plan or outline for your team to understand how you envision these Pillars to stand and operate for your business this is at least a foundation. It gives you something to look at regularly and so your team can build on it every day. This will fuel the organic growth and development of amazing ideas and team collaboration within your business.

Fuel that fire with your customers and your team every day, but always remember to let that fire breath and catch carefully so it spreads evenly across the company. Regardless of how you value the importance of work in your own life, it comprises a huge chunk of our lives: 40+ hours per week = 2,000+ hours per year!

Assuming that we are all lucky enough to have a 30 or 40+ year career making deals squeal, that's nearly 60,000 to 80,000 hours that we are at work together.

Please remember to Make Happiness a Habit folks!

Alphabet Soup of CX Terms Discussed In This Book

Agent Availability Rates: The number of agents that are available to answer customer phone calls compared to the actual phone call volume.

AI: Artificial Intelligence

CAC: Customer Acquisition Costs

Call Abandonment Rates: The percentage of inbound phone calls made to a call center or service desk that is abandoned by the customer before speaking to an agent.

CES: Customer Effort Score. Way to measure customer satisfaction by asking one single question.

Chatbots: Computer programs designed to simulate a conversation with a human user.

CI: Continuous Improvement, closely related to Six Sigma.

CJM: Customer Journey Map is a detailed outline of the steps your customers take during their experience with your company.

CLV: Customer Lifetime Value

CRM: Customer Relationship Management tool

CS: Customer Success

CSAT: Customer Satisfaction. A measure of how products and services supplied by a company meet or surpass customer satisfaction.

Customer Churn: When customers cease their relationship with your company. Also known as customer attrition.

Customer Retention: The ability for a company to keep its customers for a specific period of time.

CX: Customer Experience

CXC: CXChronicles is a customer experience and service design consultancy.

CX Nation: The CXC Podcast listenership.

Design Thinking: Refers to the cognitive, strategic and practical processes by which design concepts are developed by designers and/or design teams.

Detractor: In NPS scoring, Detractors gave a score lower or equal to 6. They are not particularly thrilled by the product or the service.

DTMF: Dual Tone Multifrequency is the signal to the phone company that you generate when you press a phone's touch keys.

ENPS: Employee Net Promoter Score

Escalation Paths: Procedure to insure that when problems can't be resolved within an agreed time frame, they are rapidly brought to the appropriate level of responsibility for adequate resolution.

First Contact Rates: The period of time it takes a customer to first connect with your company.

ICP: Ideal Customer Profile

Issue Resolution Time: The period of time that it takes your business to resolve a customer issue.

IVR: Interactive Voice Response is a technology that allows a computer to interact with humans through the use of voice and DTMF tones.

KPIs: Key Performance Indicators are performance metrics that evaluate the success of an organization or of a particular activity in which it engages.

LTV: Lifetime Value

MHAH: Make Happiness a Habit!

MRR: Monthly Recurring Revenue

NPS: The Net Promoter Score is an index ranging from -100 to 100 that measures the willingness of customers to recommend a company's products or services to others.

NCP: Non-ideal customer profiles -- the types of customers that might not be best suited for your business.

Organizational Chart: A diagram that shows the structure of an organization and the relationships and relative ranks of its parts and positions/jobs

OKR (Objective Key Result): a framework for defining and tracking objectives and their outcomes.

Passive: In NPS scoring, 'Passives' gave a score of 7 or 8. They are somewhat satisfied but could easily switch to a competitor's offering if given the opportunity.

Pillar One - Team: The fundamentals related to your team or overall organizational structure

Pillar Two - Tools: The fundamentals related to tools, systems or software that your company uses to serve its customers.

Pillar Three - Process: The fundamentals related to the working processes and workflows that guide your business and help to guide your team, customers and partners on a daily basis.

Pillar Four - Feedback: The fundamental related to the intricacies of customer- and employee-based feedback.

Promoter: In NPS scoring, 'Promoters' answered 9 or 10. They love the company's products and services.

Process Map: A planning and management tool that visually describes the flow of work.

SOPs: Standard Operating Procedures (sometimes referred to as a 'living playbook') are a set of step-by-step instructions compiled by an organization to help workers carry out complex routine operations.

SWOT Analysis: A technique for understanding your Strengths and Weaknesses, and for identifying both the Opportunities open to you and the Threats you face.

Toolkits: The resources including software that a team uses on a daily basis to serve their function.

UX: User Experience -- the overall experience a specific user has for your brand, service or mission.

VOC: the Voice of the Customer is the overall feeling or sentiment that your customer base has for your brand or company.

VOC: Voice of the Employee is the overall feeling or sentiment that your employee base has for your brand or company.

VOP: Voice of Partner is the way that your partners feel about your brand or company.

Websites and Additional Works Sourced For This Book:

1. Live chat software solutions 2019 -- https://www.crazyegg.com/blog/live-chat-software-solutions/

2. 99 Firms stats about LinkedIn 2019 -- https://99firms.com/blog/linkedin-statistics/

3. Twitter Stats 2019 -- https://www.oberlo.com/blog/twitter-statistics

4. Instagram Stats 2019 -- https://www.oberlo.com/blog/instagram-stats-every-marketer-should-know

5. Facebook Stats 2019 -- https://www.statista.com/statistics/264810/number-of-monthly-active-facebook-users-worldwide/

6. IT Support Levels 2019 -- https://www.bmc.com/blogs/support-levels-level-1-level-2-level-3/

7. 55 Amazing Stats about Slack -- https://expandedramblings.com/index.php/slack-statistics/

8. Design Thinking Basics -- https://en.wikipedia.org/wiki/Design_thinking

9. Pointillist -- https://www.pointillist.com/blog/

10. Medallia -- https://www.medallia.com/blog/page/2/

11. Gainsight -- https://www.gainsight.com/customer-success-management/

12. Teletech -- https://www.ttec.com/resources/blog

13. Salesforce -- https://www.salesforce.com/blog/

14. Zendesk -- https://www.zendesk.com/blog/

15. Twilio -- https://www.twilio.com/blog

Made in the USA
Monee, IL
15 June 2021